JACK BLACK

ROCK 'N' ROLL, COMEDY & KUNG FU

Published in 2009 by
INDEPENDENT MUSIC PRESS
Independent Music Press is an imprint of I.M. P. Publishing Limited

Jack Black – Rock 'n' Roll, Comedy & Kung Fu
by Ben Welch

British Library Cataloguing-in-Publication Data.
A catalogue for this book is available from The British Library.
ISBN: 978-1-906191-08-5

Cover Design by Fresh Lemon.
Cover photograph by Matt Baron/BEI/Rex Features

Printed in the UK.

Independent Music Press
P.O. Box 69,
Church Stretton, Shropshire
SY6 6WZ
Visit us on the web at: www.impbooks.com
and www.myspace.com/independentmusicpress
For a free catalogue, e-mail us at: info@impbooks.com
Fax: 01694 720049

Jack Black

Rock 'n' Roll, Comedy & Kung Fu

by Ben Welch

Independent Music Press

CONTENTS

ACKNOWLEDGEMENTS

My sincere gratitude to any and all who have offered support, encouragement and/or distraction. Many thanks to Martin for the faith and the opportunity; to Mum, Dad and Krystal for putting up with the tantrums; and to the Coach House Massive for always taking an interest.

INTRODUCTION

It's mid-November, 2006, and the illustrious Four Seasons Hotel in Beverly Hills is playing host to some distinctly ribald high jinks. This is because the band Tenacious D are in residence, currently running the press gauntlet to promote their latest release, a movie entitled *Tenacious D in The Pick of Destiny*, and its accompanying soundtrack. Behind the door of the fifteenth floor master suite, you might be forgiven for expecting talk of multi-million dollar deals or cloak-and-dagger political jostling. Less usual, one suspects, is a 37-year-old man pulling down his trousers and underwear, squatting, and enthusiastically farting. It's not that this is especially senseless – "I want to keep those pants clean," perpetrator Jack Black explains, and he might be onto something. But it is symptomatic of the fact that Black has never been entirely in synch with Hollywood's leading man archetype, in appearance, in behaviour, or in output. And yet, leading man he most certainly is: in performance, in exposure, and in bank balance.

Today, jostling and joking with band-mate Kyle Gass for the benefit of an *LA Weekly* journalist, he is every bit the manic, hyper-animated comedic dynamo that has made him such a valuable commodity in movies. But in the mercilessly fickle entertainment arena, it is not his gurning, growling on-screen persona that has cemented his place as a key player; rather, his versatility. On this occasion he is promoting not only a film, as its lead actor, co-writer and executive producer, but also a record. Many actors have woefully misjudged the deceptive chasm between film and music, but Black has not only traversed it, he has dovetailed the two together, blurring the distinction between stage and screen, creating a niche that other ill-fated thespians-cum-minstrels can only dream of. Tenacious D is no mere side-project; it is the foundation on which Black has built his career.

Jokingly mocking what he calls the "lefty, non-linear" patter of the interview, Kyle Gass leaves the suite to attend to some other business. While the journalist is in the bathroom, and confronted with the still running Dictaphone, Black decides to perform an impromptu monologue. Soon his musings bring him onto his career. "Early on, when you're young," he declares, "you think, 'Yeah, I'm gonna get in there and do some movies or something. I'll break into the industry club, and I'll fuckin' know how it works and what it's about.' But then you get in there and you realise there's no real club or industry, or any rhyme or reason. Everyone's just floatin' around, doin' weird jobs, and it's a very fuckin' random, Nietzschean universe of fuckin' endless, empty, mindless destruction."

What is the reader to make of this? Is it substance? Is it a spoof of sincerity? Perhaps it's substance masquerading as spoofed sincerity, or the other way around. It's not just the Hollywood prototype that Black is at odds with. At times he seems at odds with himself, his larger than life persona suspended in an uneasy tension with a quieter, more reserved aspect to his character – one that zealously guards his private life. Perhaps this is how Black has carried off straight roles with the same conviction and ability that has made him a comedy star. As his band mate Gass once profoundly noted, you can't have an orgasm without friction.

Gass returns as the interview ends, seemingly nonplussed about the monologue he just missed. Black insists that it's going to win the reporter a Pulitzer, or even the Nobel Peace Prize. The next round of interviewers bustle in the hall outside, and the press junket thunders on, oblivious to the soliloquy that possibly was (but probably wasn't) a major achievement.

It does, however, raise a point – his story might not have any rhyme or reason, it might be fuckin' empty, endless, and mindless. But it's still a story.

Chapter 1

FOR COMEDY AND EXPERIMENTATION

The (in)famous Summer of Love was just two years passed when Jack Black was born Thomas Jack Black on August 28, 1969. The heady enthusiasm of a cultural movement had inspired thousands to descend on the Haight-Ashbury district of San Francisco, drawn by the lure of free music, free drugs and free love. The hippie agenda was clear: individualism and pacifism were its key tenements, and sexual and spiritual exploration were actively encouraged. In June 1967, the sense of genuine momentum and purpose was uniting hippies both regionally and internationally, and it seemed as if the Summer of Love would go on forever.

Of course, it didn't. By October, Haight-Ashbury was suffering the consequences of its participation in the movement, with homelessness, crime and drug addiction rife. It is 1969, however, that holds the particular significance of featuring both the fullest expression of the hippie movement's potential, and the event that engendered its dissolution. The former was Woodstock festival, held in the state of New York, an event that boasted some of the most legendary artists of all-time on a single bill. The likes of Janis Joplin, The Who, Neil Young and Jimi Hendrix gathered to perform for a crowd of tens of thousands (many of these artists would influence Jack Black significantly throughout his childhood). Despite many sections of the media wishing to portray the event as a lawless exercise in excess, the reports coming from the festival told a different story. They told of a remarkable air of community, solidarity and compassion; one *New York Times* reporter memorably called it "a beautiful and amazing accident." By contrast, The Altamont Free Concert, held in northern California in December, was not so benign an affair. Billed as 'Woodstock West', tragedy struck during the Rolling Stone's performance; 18-year old Meredith Hunter was reportedly killed by one of the Hell's Angels who had been hired as security for the show, and the media had found all the ammunition they could ever want to discredit the hippie movement.

And so, it was into this atmosphere that Jack Black was born. The ideals and aspirations of the Summer of Love remained, but the innocence of the movement had been forever sullied. The hangover of the 1970s, and the compromised permissiveness left behind from the late 1960s, was to have a personal bearing on young Jack's life. He was born the first and only child of Judith and Thomas William Black – his mother had three children from a previous marriage, and his father a further one. How his parents met is unclear, though; Black believes that it was most likely as a result of their shared passion for folk dancing. The first ten years of his life were spent in Hermosa Beach, California. This affluent and glamorous city records some of the highest house prices in the US, and the beach itself – its name meaning "beautiful" in Spanish – is a renowned hot spot for surfing and beach volleyball.

Judith and Thomas worked together as satellite engineers, or, of you will, rocket scientists. His mother worked on the Hubble Space Telescope – a giant telescope launched in 1990 to take images of the furthest reaches of the solar system. Black maintains that he has never fully understood what they were doing, simply imagining "a lot of mathematical equations and chalkboards and stuff". Similarly mysterious is how two people in such a technical, specialised profession begot the child that would grow into Jack Black; "I got the 'rock' science," he suggested to Mark Binelli of *Rolling Stone*, "but not the 'et.'" What is clear is that Black spent a lot of time entertaining himself as a child, perhaps due to the abundance of step-siblings that inevitably jostled for airspace in the family home, or perhaps simply due to his dynamic imagination. His childhood features the same pattern of eccentric activity, from absurdity to achievement, that has defined his adulthood career. He recalls that from a young age he craved attention, and quickly figured out that acting was a fine means of obtaining it. His first taste followed a Passover Seder (the Jewish feast commemorating the freedom of the Israelites from Egyptian slavery) where the family played games of role-play and imagination. Despite not having access to a video camera, he also liked to star in his own imaginary short films; he would act out his own scenes, inspired by his love of the classic 1970s show *The Six Million Dollar Man,* mimicking the hero Steve Austin or one of his various adversaries. It was a schooling that would serve him well, but it wasn't just privately that he would entertain these fantasies. Black also remembers threading wires up his sleeves, wanting them to be just visible enough to pique the curiosity of his friends and classmates: then at the crucial moment, when suspicion was at its most fervent, he would hide them, explaining their existence away, reasoning that a cyborg would want to hide his synthetic nature.

Building on these mini-performances, the young Jack decided to document his talent. He started performing radio plays, skits and sketches, and recorded them onto tape. It was to be a persistent practice – one that would continue into his teens and ultimately bear considerable fruit. But not all of his activities were quite so productive. He also had a Rottweiler-Bull Mastiff cross named Chico, who he would subject to trials of speed and intelligence: building mazes from chairs, couches and cushions, he would force his companion to run the gauntlet. Sliding down the stairs in a sleeping bag was another well-established childhood pastime that Jack regularly enjoyed. More bizarrely, on one occasion he decided to put cocoa puffs in the crack of his rectum. At six or seven, he remembers, "cocoa puffs in the butt was about the funniest thing that could possibly happen." But it was not just the humour of the scenario that incited this act of bodily vandalism: "For comedy *and* experimentation. I was a scientist!" Perhaps he did inherit something from his parents after all.

Jack's father Thomas converted to Judaism upon marrying Judith, and being raised Jewish, Jack had to attend Hebrew school three times a week during this period. It was an obligation he did not regard fondly. It failed to arouse his interest at all, and he resented having to study more than the other kids at his school. Jack spent a lot of his time at school asleep anyway – he remembers on one occasion waking up in a different lesson as all his classmates had left – so more school was never about to incite his enthusiasm. Indeed, it's a predilection he has carried into his adult life, noting that if a film feels like it has an educational bent, he will generally doze off. The combination of this boredom and his lust for attention also meant he would often act up at school, playing the class clown. "I wanted to be laughed at and I wasn't very funny. It took years of wanting to be funny before anything funny happened." At the age of eight, Jack got his first taste of acting proper, while he was away at Summer Camp. He was cast in a production of *The Wizard of Oz*, in no less than the title role; from this point on, he continued to star in as many amateur productions as time would allow. His talents had been noted for the first time of many.

It was at this time that Jack also started being interested in music, though he had not yet discovered the joys of rock that would later become such an identifiable part of his persona. His first love were Swedish pop ambassadors, ABBA, upon hearing their 1977 hit, 'Take A Chance On Me'.

As Jack's age approached double figures, his parents' relationship began to show signs of strain; when their tempers flared, Jack would often run to the housekeeper for reassurance, who had a son, Juan, his age – welcome company in these times of tension. But as time wore on, the situation became more desperate and the phantom of the Summer of Love intervened to further complicate matters.

The Blacks visited a club based in Huntington Beach, southern California, called Family Synergy, whose website states it is a "place to explore alternatives to traditional monogamy in a warm, supportive, humanistic atmosphere." Buzzwords here include "polyamory" or "polyfidelty", but definitely not "swinging", due to a focus on deeper relationships. At any rate, Black recalls "synergizing with all these families", and seems to remain somewhat bemused by the whole experience. After meeting a woman at the camp, they returned to live in Hermosa Beach, with the new partner sleeping in the same bed as Judith and Thomas. Though merely an attempt to save their marriage, Black remembers it as a "meltdown." The third participant in the relationship left, but it was too late to save the marriage. With Jack ten years old, Thomas left Judith, moving a mile away with a new girlfriend. Sadly the problems were not over. Jack's mother struggled with the split and there were fiery confrontations with the new girlfriend. Not only this, but Jack felt a strong attraction to his father's new partner, even stealing some suggestive pictures Thomas had taken of her. When she later left, Jack wondered if his infatuation was the cause of the break-up, though he also acknowledges that this was potentially a projection of his own anxiety.

Black's parents have both since remarried, but this experience had a marked effect on Jack. Speaking to *GQ* in January 2006, he said: "If you're growing up and you have two sides of yourself, your mother's and your father's, that don't like each other and break up, then this side of yourself doesn't like that side of yourself, and there's a constant disharmony that comes from that." But despite the difficulties he undoubtedly faced, he has expressed his gladness that his parents were able to move on, and insists that the episode was not a big deal. He speaks affectionately of the different characteristics he has inherited from both parents: from his mother, a fierce temper and dislike of seeing blood or injury; and from his father, a love of walking, pork chops and corn, and pondering the nature of infinity. Quite a combination.

Following his parent's eventual divorce, aged ten years old, he moved from Hermosa Beach with his mother to Culver City – some fifteen miles down the road. This new setting was to have a considerable bearing on Jack's teenage years. It had also been the birthplace of Oscar-winning actress Helen Hunt, who Jack would star alongside in *Bob Roberts* thirteen years after his arrival. Significantly, Culver City was and still is known as 'the Heart of Screenland"; since the 1920s it had been a site of major importance for the film industry, due largely to the MGM Film Studios being situated right in its centre. Indeed, it was the location for the 1939 MGM production of *The Wizard of Oz*, a film Black was most familiar with since his Summer Camp excursion. In 1979, when Jack arrived, the well-worn studio system of filmmaking was in decline, however, and MGM chose to sell much of its property for redevelopment. Nonetheless, the city remained a crucial site of film production and Jack was surrounded by the bustle and tumult of the entertainment industry at its most vital.

With his parents both being high level scientists and enjoying very well-paid jobs, Jack and his mother were able to move into a large eight-bedroom house, many rooms of which his mum rented out to lodgers. One of these lodgers happened to be a journalist, though not that Jack really cared; he was initially far more interested in his dog, capable of catching Frisbees, mid-flight. But this journalist was ultimately to spark Jack's enthusiasm for music, introducing him to his two favourite artists: willowy soft-rockers Fleetwood Mac and folk troubadours Simon and Garfunkel. He also admits an enduring love for Bobby McFerrin, the son of opera singer Robert McFerrin. Bobby famously wrote and performed the first *a cappella* song to ever reach Number 1 in the US, *Don't Worry, Be Happy* (though Black insists that he was a fan before this track highlighted McFerrin to the mainstream consciousness). McFerrin's vocal flexibility allows him to perform entire songs and complex arrangements using his voice alone, and this struck a chord with a young, attention-hungry Black. He envisaged commanding the stage alone, wowing the audience with his singular talent. Drawing further on his love of Dr. Seuss (the surreal American writer and cartoonist) he had heard being read on record, he pictured himself performing solo compositions, with different parts of the harmony emerging from different parts of his face. He even remembers going to see McFerrin in concert, where he was invited up on stage to perform in a crowd participation segment of the show, enthusiastically slapping his chest in time to the music. He also enjoyed a glimpse behind the curtains with eccentric new wavers Devo; his older brother Howard Siegel had worked as an engineer on their 1980 platinum album, *Freedom of Choice*. He had taken Jack to see the band perform live in Santa Monica, the first concert he had ever been to. One imagines, however, that a young lad most at ease with the po-faced strains of Simon and Garfunkel would find the angular rhythms and dissonance of Devo somewhat unsettling.

With this cautious yet eclectic foray into the world of pop music, Jack's tastes were to rapidly tend toward rock. His first purchase was *The Grand Illusion*, the breakthrough record for hard rock veterans Styx and their first triple platinum album. Its commercialised progressive styling, combining the experimentalism and grandiosity of British prog bands with catchy choruses and hooks, soon led Jack on to the likes of Journey; and so begins a tale that Black himself acknowledges has become personal mythology. Or rather, the tale begins in 1979, when Ozzy Osbourne left heavy metal forefathers Black Sabbath and thereafter assembled a new project with the help of wife Sharon. With former Rainbow bassist Bob Daisley, Ozzy set about the task of writing and recording a new album. And in January 1981, Ozzy released his debut record as a solo artist, entitled *Blizzard of Ozz*. The release of this milestone in the heavy metal canon fortuitously combined with a pushy record store employee, who dissuaded an eleven year-old boy from buying a Journey album – instead handing him *Blizzard of Ozz* and instructing him to buy it instead. Jack Black remembers that event fondly. He liked the guy's T-shirt and was naturally drawn to 'big brother' figures, and as such yielded. "That album changed my life," he remarked in the *Independent on Sunday.* Black was well on his way to becoming the rock 'n' roll aficionado he is known as today.

Just as his music tastes were gaining definition and forming, so too was his taste in film. His early love of *The Six Million Dollar Man* proved abiding, and it was science fiction that Jack found most engaging as a pre-teen boy. Today he still heaps praise on George Miller's *Mad Max 2: The Road Warrior*, the 1981 sequel to the film that launched Mel Gibson. Drawing on well-worn Western themes, the film concerns a group of settlers who are forced to defend themselves against a marauding band of outlaws. Perhaps Black was most drawn to Gibson, who described his performance as "Heavy Metal acting, doing less and making more out of it." But Jack maintains that his favourite film as a child was Arthur Hiller's 1976 remake of *Silver Streak*. In this suspenseful comedy, a man is forced to enlist the assistance of a criminal in order to prove the innocence of the woman he loves. Gene Wilder and Richard Pryor star, two actors who Black admired hugely in his childhood. There are echoes of Wilder in many of Black's performances today – the combination of a tremendous physicality and animation with a disarmingly wide-eyed innocence.

At the age of thirteen, as is Jewish custom, Jack Black became a Bar Mitzvah. With this, he became of age and was hence considered an adult: "One to whom the commandments apply." With this newfound responsibility, Jack was able to exercise more control over his religious life – and immediately decided to abandon Judaism. Hebrew School had been a constant encumbrance to him and he endeavoured to waste no more of his time. "As I was a man," he told Ed Potton of *The Times Online*, "I decided never to go to synagogue again." It was also around this time that he first began dabbling proactively in music, though his aspirations were initially cut very short. His first fleeting tenure as the singer in an unnamed rock band was disastrous. He was in High School and taking his rock as seriously as any teen would care to. During one party, his band launched into a cover of the Black Sabbath classic 'Iron Man', only to realise that no one was actually paying any attention to them. Disheartened, the band gave up half way through the performance, packing away their instruments and leaving. While it may seem little more than a cute anecdote in light of his later success, it was an experience that was devastating for Black at the time, and one that ended his musical aspirations for many years – until he joined forces with Kyle Gass, in fact. But before that most auspicious meeting of talents would herald a new force in the rock arena, Black had some considerable hurdles to overcome.

For now, Black was more tied up in acting and somehow even managed to secure himself a paid role. His first job was in 1982, the same year as his Bar Mitzvah when he was only 13. Indeed, he had prayed to God asking for a television appearance to impress his friends; and God couldn't have been too irked about Black's defection from Judaism, because he came through magnificently. It was every young boy's dream – a commercial for the Activision videogame, *Pitfall!,* on the Atari 2600 console. A decidedly fresher faced and leaner Jack than the public are accustomed to seeing appears, clad in khakis and a safari hat. But what is familiar is his excitability, clenching his fists emphatically as he declares, "Just last night I was lost in the jungle with Pitfall Harry, surrounded by giant scorpions and man eating crocodiles!" By all accounts, his friends and classmates were overcome with admiration. More work followed this rousing success, but unfortunately for Jack, it was for a considerably less glamorous product – Smurfberry Crunch cereal. Even a chance to star alongside the famous blue-skinned sprites couldn't redeem the gig, and it was an appearance he thought he'd never live down; "My stock plummeted at school. *Pitfall!* was cool. Being in a Smurfberry Crunch cereal ad and being pulled along by a red wagon…?"

Regardless of his credibility in the playground, Jack was moving in the right direction. He followed this with a small part in *The Fall Guy*, an early-to-mid-1980s TV series. Here he got the chance to at least share a studio with the inimitable Lee Majors – the man who had played his childhood hero, Colonel Steve Austin, in *The Six Million Dollar Man*. In *The Fall Guy*, Majors played Colt Seavers, a stunt man who improbably tided himself over by bounty hunting. For the first time Black had been credited alongside one of his heroes, and it was a trend set to continue.

There is one more performance that is particularly noteworthy in this brief pre-history. Black was next cast in a small play entitled *Inside Eddie Bienstock,* a project that had been developed by a radical acting troupe called The Actors' Gang. The director was a young Tim Robbins, a Theatre Studies student at UCLA, at this point unknown. Black's mum would drop him off at the theatre every day, but the rigours of theatre acting was not to be for the young man at this stage – three weeks into the six-week run, he left the production. Unbeknownst to the twelve-year-old Jack, The Actors' Gang, and Tim Robbins would prove hugely important in his development. For the time being, he was glad to get back to his videogames.

As he grew older, Jack's mind turned to other things. His ascent to international fame was not to be without its obstacles, and come the age of fifteen, he had developed a rebellious streak that was threatening to take over his life. As young as eleven he had been experimenting with soft drugs, or at least, attempting to. He bought some cannabis with his friends and smoked it on the roof of his garage, though they later agreed that it was almost certainly just tea leaves. By thirteen he had begun mixing with fellow metal fans at school and around Culver City. He was partaking in many of the activities that teens with a propensity to rebel do; he began drinking beer and smoking cigarettes, and then moved on to smoking cannabis (this time sure of what it was). He and his friends would hang around on the streets, scattering when they saw a police car, regardless of whether or not it was actually interested in them.

However, things soon escalated and became more serious. Jack admits to doing cocaine after "falling in with some rough dudes" and, as he explained to www.moviecrazed.com, he also tried acid for the first time. What's more, he had kissed a girl involved with a less than upstanding character, a "motorcycle gang guy." While bike-riding miscreants terrorising the general public sounds a lot like the plot of *The Road Warrior*, Black himself was no Mad Max. He had only been in one fight before, at the age of twelve, when a playground bully had singled him out for a fight out of sheer malevolence. Despite his protestations of being a lover, not a fighter, the kid continued his advance, determined to administer a beating – at which point, as Black says, "my Judo skills kicked in, and I flipped him! I felt bad about it, but at the same time, I also felt good about it."

Unfortunately, on this occasion, some rudimentary knowledge of Judo was not going to stop him getting a thrashing. The delinquent had already beaten him up once – "not too badly," in his own words – but undoubtedly bad enough to give him a fright. More concerning was the fact that the grievance wasn't yet laid to rest, and his rival was coming back for more, claiming he wanted to kill Jack. Perhaps we came close to having no Jack Black at all.

But the final straw came when, short on cash, a friend stole his mother's credit card to buy cocaine. Unbeknownst to Jack, his so-called pal also used the card to go on a shopping spree, and when his parents found out, they decided action had to be taken. Looking back at this period, Jack reflects that he was "on a rampage", and by fifteen, "in full meltdown". Perhaps the fallout of his parent's divorce exacerbated this descent. He states that he "was really searching for a father figure", and this is why he associated himself with such a questionable crowd. Despite his father being present and supportive during this time, he told Simmy Richman of *The Independent* that "for some reason

I wished that I had a Harley-Davidson riding heavy metal dad, and that's what I went to find." Unfortunately, what he also found was drug use and threats of violence, and when his parents declared that he was being pulled out of school, he was relieved rather than resistant.

The school he was subsequently placed in was quite a change from the public (comprehensive) inner city establishment he had been used to. His parents chose to send him to The Poseidon School in West LA, a non-public day school specialising in teaching children who have not flourished in the conventional education system; as their website states, they are meeting "the unique needs of adolescents who are bright but have learning, emotional and/or social problems." Established in 1971, one of the corner stones of the Poseidon approach is a flexible schedule, and at the time of Black's arrival, there were only around twenty other students enrolled. It was an experience that Black recalls as "intense", as he was surrounded by a small group of teens who had, for the most part, been expelled from their schools. However, it was a vital step, and one that proved wholly successful. Other, more troubled students at the school were going to see the on-campus therapist every day, and Black's curiosity led him to ask if he too could receive some therapy. The first session that he received is called to mind somewhat hazily, but without doubt enthusiastically. Black simply started confessing all his wrongdoings – he was allegedly backed up with guilt due to the absence of confession from Judaism – and regaled the therapist with the tale of his first experimentations with drugs, through to his use of harder substances, the incident with the gang member, and finally his part in the theft of his mum's credit card. He recalls crying and crying until he could cry no more, and emerging from the therapist's office feeling like a new man.

And while his acting career may have been put on hold for a while by his waywardness, being at Poseidon not only reignited the passion but also stoked it to new heights. He claims that it was this period in particular when he really began considering acting as a career. "I realised then," he remarks, "for the most part, I really liked being in the limelight for some insecure reason." While studying at Poseidon he had the good fortune to be taught drama by one Debbie Devine. Debbie is herself established and highly respected as an actress, director and producer, and is currently the artistic director of the 24th Street Theatre in LA. She is also the founder and artistic director of the Glorious Repertory Co., which works principally out of the 24th Street Theatre. And despite saying that he has had many acting coaches that have served as mentors throughout his training, it is Debbie's words to Jack that have stayed at the forefront of his mind. Jack recalls her questioning his ambitions, saying: "Hey, why do you want to be an actor? Why don't you be a writer or director? Those people are the ones who are really the brains behind the movies. Why do you just want to be a puppet?" While these words may sound suspiciously like discouragement, Black saw it differently. He felt that he was being told to write his own ticket; to not rely on the success of others to carry him forward, as on the crest of a wave, but to be actively involved in the formation of his own wave. Considering the steady but tireless rise of Tenacious D, and how closely linked his success as an actor has been linked to it, it seems that Debbie Devine was talking a lot of sense.

Encouraged by Debbie Devine as well as his rediscovered love of acting, Black began attending theatre productions more regularly. On one occasion he saw one of his heroes, American actor John Malkovich, in a production in LA. "Like anyone," he told Ed Potton, "I've been reduced to a trembling idiot around people I really admire." This occasion was no different; Black remembers Malkovich's reticence to shake his hand, but is sympathetic – he has since been in the same position countless times, where fans are jostling for his attention but he simply wants to disappear.

With his behaviour under control and his life seemingly back on track, Jack was eventually able to leave behind the ultimately fulfilling experience that Poseidon provided for him. His parents had stopped paying for therapy which he no longer required (after the first one-off), and he had a mind to furthering his skills as an actor, so he applied to the Crossroads School, in Santa Monica, in 1984. He was immediately accepted, for which he considers himself very fortunate; it was, as he says, a "great school" – and one, no doubt, that it is not at all easy to get into. But a quick glance at its alumni will reveal that, if acting is where your passions lie, Crossroads School is the foremost choice of institution. Amongst its graduates are Hollywood heavyweight Michael Bay, director of *Transformers*, *Pearl Harbour* and the *Bad Boys* films; actor Sean Astin, best known as Samwise Gamgee in the *Lord of the Rings* trilogy; Kate Hudson, who won a Golden Globe and was nominated for an Oscar for her role in *Almost Famous*; and Gwyneth Paltrow, who would later star alongside Black in *Shallow Hal*.

The Crossroads School is well known in the States as a progressive, liberal private school – one that is particularly esteemed for its arts-based curricula. The current headmaster, Roger Weaver, states on the website *www.xrds.org* that "we consider the expressive and creative qualities of children to be as significant as the essential cognitive skills they need to develop." In this vein, the drama course is particularly renowned as one of the finest in the country, developing improvisational skills and formal technique, as well as providing an overview of the history of theatre. The school also offers no fewer than four film courses. Perhaps this approach goes some way to explaining how Crossroads has developed so many successful performing artists; understandably, all of this fine training comes at a price. Today the fees for the school stand at around $22,000 per academic year.

During his time at Crossroads, Jack was under the tutelage of a writer and performer called R. A. White whom, it later transpired, was also a member of the aforementioned Actors' Gang that had produced *Inside Eddie Bienstock*. That year he was working on a play called *'The Big Show'* alongside another Actors' Gang regular, Michael Schlitt. Schlitt remembers Black well, a young man who used to hang around in White's home reading rather than go back to his own house after school. "He was like a fixture," he commented in *The Jewish Journal*. "He was very quiet." According to Schlitt, White had noticed Black's talent, and remarked that they ought to find a place for him in an Actors' Gang production. Clearly, his earlier defection from the cast of *Inside Eddie Bienstock* had not worked against him. He was now offered the role of an anonymous soldier in *The Big Show*, and upon accepting he happened to meet, amongst others, a man named Kyle Gass.

Chapter 2

KYLE GASS AND THE ACTORS' GANG

Kyle Gass debuted in the world on June 14, 1960, a full nine years and two months before Jack Black. He was born in Castro Valley, around 370 miles from Black's birthplace, but soon moved to Walnut Creek where he was raised. He spent his childhood with his brothers, Mitchell and Matthew, and his parents; his mother worked as a dental hygienist, his father as a fireman. He described himself as an advanced child, saying on the unofficial but excellent fan-site *www.tenaciousjoes.com* that: "I was quite precocious actually, I thought all the kids around me were pretty immature. I wore glasses and thought I was smart and talented you know, but then I sort of got more into sports and became more of a renaissance character, aiming to excel in many different areas." And fortunately for the world of tongue-in-cheek rock-folk, one of the fields the self-proclaimed "renaissance" boy decided to try his hand at was music. At eight he began playing the flute, but by twelve, he had made the wise decision to switch to a nylon string guitar, realising that the flute was unlikely to make him more popular with girls. His progress was rapid, and he doesn't shy away from pointing this out himself: "I remember playing at home and thinking, 'Wow – I'm too good to be playing at home.'" He describes his first record purchase as an "agonising tug-of-war" between The Beach Boys and funk-rock pioneers Sly And The Family Stone. He ultimately decided to go for The Beach Boys' *Endless Summer*, a collection of early hits that reached Number 1 in the US. "Interestingly enough," he noted in *The Independent On Sunday*, "I never went back and got the Sly." His first concert, some years later, was sister rock act Heart; the support, a pre-*Addicted To Love* Robert Palmer.

It's at this point that Gass' history becomes somewhat puzzling. According to one report, at a young age he was snapped up by the illustrious Julliard Music School – one of the world's finest performing arts conservatories, based in New York. Gass himself claimed, during an appearance on US chat show *Late Night With Conan O'Brien*, that he had graduated age thirteen with a degree in classical guitar studies. Black himself also enjoyed flirting with this rumour, once telling *The Times* that he was the youngest ever graduate of the Julliard music school. "The Philharmonic of literally every major city in the world was fine wining and dining him to come and play classical string guitar," he claimed, "and he opted for a road less travelled." Were this the case, Gass would have a list of fellow alumni that would even trump Jack Black's: be-bop pioneer Miles Davies and fellow band member Chick Corea, two-time Oscar winner Kevin Spacey, and Superman himself, Christopher Reeve. Unfortunately for the shelf-life of the rumour, Julliard did not have an undergraduate course for Classical Guitar Studies until 2007, a full 34 years after Gass had claimed to graduate. It soon emerged that Gass' original statement was intended as a throw-away gag that had subsequently spiralled out of control. Later, while a guest on *The Adam Carolla Radio Show* in LA, he took the opportunity to set the record straight. When asked if he attended Julliard, he replied, "I didn't, you know, I made that up as a joke … I thought it would be hilarious, and then I've been hearing about it ever since. Apologies to Julliard."

In fact, Gass attended the Las Lomas High School in northern California, graduating in 1978. It was while studying here that he got his first professional work as an actor, and much like Jack, it was in the world of commercials. He remembers meetings with "a commercial agent that lived in 'The Valley,'" more commonly known as the San Fernando Valley in LA. The agent managed to get Kyle an audition, and despite it being the first one he had ever attended, he got the part. "I just auditioned and felt it," he remembers. Unfortunately, the hard evidence of his first starring role has since been lost forever – by Gass. He took the one remaining copy from his mother to take care of, but subsequently misplaced the videotape. As such, the only record remaining is from Gass' memory: "I played kind of a slacker waiter who walks into a restaurant with a bunch of attitude to the tune of 'Wild Thing'… I think I look like I'm about thirteen in it." From this humble beginning, he decided to further his talents as an actor at university. He went to study at the University of California, Los Angles, or UCLA as it is more commonly known. It is here that his career truly began to take shape; but first, another story needs to briefly be told.

Gass was studying Theatre alongside Tim Robbins, who in 1979 was part of an intra-mural softball team. Playing alongside other Theatre Studies students, their course title was mistaken for their team name; humiliated by the prospect of such a fey tag in such a masculine environment, they changed their name to the ironically excessive 'Male Death Cult', and adopted a skull and crossed baseball bats as their logo. But they soon found that they had more in common than a love of running around fields chasing a ball. Robbins had been writing and directing plays since he was a teenager, and with the noise of the Cold War and Reagan's arms race droning in the background, Robbins resolved to bring some noise of his own into theatre; the anger and activism of punk rock. In 1981, as part of his course, Robbins staged a production of *Ubu The King*, a play written by the

Frenchman Alfred Jarry, originally titled *Ubu Roi*. This play not only launched the soon-to-be-christened Actors' Gang – it was so popular that all involved were intent to stage it again. The project also neatly set out their manifesto. As a work often considered precursory to the absurdist and surrealist movements, it rages vehemently against established hierarchical structures, shamelessly represents violence and crudity, and managed to provoke a riot during its 1896 premiere. Robbins simply remembers it as "wild, funny stuff."

Over the next few years, The Actors' Gang began to build up a head of steam, particularly after Robbins' graduation from UCLA in 1981 allowed him to devote more and more time to his passion project. Of course, he wasn't operating alone; two other figures that reappear in Jack Black's chronology – R. A. White and Michael Schlitt – were also running with Robbins and The Actors' Gang. Over the next few years, they continued to stage hugely successful productions, many penned by Robbins himself alongside other members.

It was 1984 when the Gang were working on *The Big Show* – a "political thing about El Salvador" or a "comic look at the Nicaraguan situation", depending on whether you ask Black or Gass, respectively. By this time, Gass was a fully integrated member of The Actors' Gang, and was working on music for the production. With Jack hanging around at R. A. White's house, it was recommended to Michael Schlitt that they involve the aspiring actor in the play. Schlitt agreed, and remembers telling White, "He's got some crazy juice. He has a charisma." Once his bit part as an anonymous solider had been secured, Black's ambition allowed him to work his way into a more creative role on *The Big Show*. Tim Robbins father, Gilbert Robbins, had enjoyed some success as a folk singer – he was a late addition to 1960s group The Highwaymen. This had rubbed off on Tim as well, as Gass noted to Hugh Hart in *SFGate*: "He was sort of a frustrated music guy himself, so there was a lot of music in every production we did." Upon learning of Black's musicality, who despite not playing an instrument had written and recorded some *a capella* songs on a four-track, Robbins asked him to get involved with writing the music for the play. There was only one man to see about the music: Kyle Gass.

Gass remembers Jack's contributions to the music in the play as "some great multi-harmony stuff," no doubt heavily influenced by his love of Bobby McFerrin. Part of *The Big Show* set-up was a faux Nicaraguan game show, and Black was tasked with writing the jingles. Everyone involved was impressed with the output of such a youthful performer. "If I didn't make it in acting or rocking, I could have been a good jingle maker for commercials," Black insists. Nonetheless, it was far from plain sailing – Jack was still largely avoiding Robbins, who he feared would hold his desertion of *'Inside Eddie Bienstock'* against him (having quit three weeks into the six-week run, Black worried that Robbins might hold a grudge). Far more concerning was his supposed collaborator Gass, who was most perturbed that a newcomer, and a preciously talented one at that, was encroaching on his territory. While this was nothing new for The Actors' Gang – Robbins himself refers to it in *The Jewish Journal* as a running history of "conflicts that have risen up, people who have fallen out and egos" – it was a major obstacle for Jack. He remembers Gass being mostly hostile at first, saying: "Oh yeah, he was ice cold … I had some music I was proposing for the play. And he was the music dude in the company, so I think he felt, 'What the fuck is this bullshit? I'm the music guy.'" Gass honestly concurs with Jack's interpretation, though he phrases it with the more diplomatic, "we were not instant friends."

1984 was an important year for The Actors' Gang as well as for Jack himself. It was the year that the Summer Olympics came to Los Angeles, and with it, the Olympic Festival of the Arts. As part of the extensive program of culture that was arranged, a renowned avant-garde theatre troupe travelled from Paris: the Theatre du Soleil, or Theatre of the Sun. Much like The Actors' Gang, it was an ensemble first established at University, between the Theatre students of L'Ecole Internationale de Theatre Jacques Lecoq. Founded in 1964, it had since risen to international prominence – Schlitt remembers their reinterpretations of Shakespeare's *Richard II* and *Henry V* as "extraordinary" – and it provided an inspiring model for the ambitious UCLA students. Robbins had previously studied French with one of its principal actors, George Bigot, who now returned to run workshops with The Actors' Gang. The instruction was invaluable, his techniques allowing the Gang to find a method in their madness. "We had all the energy and the passion," remarks Robbins, "but we didn't have the form or the discipline of how to get there."

Bigot taught them a *modus operandi* that they came to call "The Style"; an immediate, confrontational methodology that demanded the audience be engaged directly. He also taught them to regard their roles as varying composites of four essential elements: happy and sad, angry and afraid. Schlitt remembers Bigot's influence as "a critical development," and one which ensured the impressive maturation of The Actors' Gang into an established, eminent ensemble.

In 1987, Black graduated from Crossroads, with some respectable experience behind him and a solid foundation in acting technique. It was also the year that The Actors' Gang staged *Violence*. Co-written by Robbins, it starred John Cusack, who would later play the lead in Black's breakthrough film, *High Fidelity*. But major movie roles were still pie in the sky for Jack, who was for the time being preoccupied with what to do next. He was sure he wanted to pursue acting as far as he could take it; the question was, where to study. In fact, it wasn't much of a question at all. UCLA had a prestigious course, and more importantly, it was the hunting ground of The Actors' Gang.

His previous work with them did not buy him immediate entry, however, so he was not yet acting with the Gang. For some time he admired from afar, attending performances and hanging around with the members he had connections with. "They were legendary at school," he remembers. "Everybody wanted to be in, y'know, it was like being in The Beatles or something." Nonetheless, he did ultimately work his way into the necessary circles and eventually began work-shopping with the Gang. Here he learnt the fundamentals of 'The Style', as well as vital creative techniques; Bigot had taught the Gang to work from an improbable starting point, developing small, improvisational techniques into larger pieces. It was this role-play that Black excelled in, having loved performing those off-the-cuff skits as a child; this technique of writing while performing, performing as you write, profoundly influenced his methods and technique when he came to write for Tenacious D.

With a whole new range of skills under his belt, Black began performing with The Actors' Gang for the first time since his brief run in *Inside Eddie Bienstock*. In marked contrast to the outrageously comic characters that would come to be his bread and butter in later life, here he was paying his dues and learning his craft by performing in some truly heavyweight plays. He recalls one Actors' Gang adaptation of the poems of Bertolt Brecht – a German poet and playwright whose works are performed more regularly in his homeland than Shakespeare's. It was "basically just a bunch of his poems that he wrote while he was in Los Angeles," Black recollected in *The Believer*, "we sang songs and did little scenes of him trying to make it in Hollywood." He also performed in a production of Eugene Ionesco's *Exit the King*, which the Gang had re-titled *Farewell to the King*. It concerns the monarch of an unnamed country who, informed of his impending death, muses on his wretchedness in the face of his own mortality. Black is not best known for his portrayal of men burdened with the weight of existential anxieties, but nonetheless, he remembers the play as "fucking great." "I like the absurd," he remarks, and as one of the leading exponents of the Theatre of the Absurd, Ionesco must have proved a stimulating challenge. While it may seem somewhat deluded to attribute too much gravitas to Black's early performances, his straight roles in later films such as *Margot At The Wedding* do demonstrate a heightened awareness of the link between tragedy and comedy. So in fact, while many more recent spectators consider some of his film choices bizarre, several of his more puzzling roles can be regarded as reverting to type rather than changing direction.

With more and more experience of meatier roles, a big opportunity was soon to come Jack's way. In 1987, Tim Robbins had been working on a play with another regular Gang cohort, Adam Simon (who had also co-written *Violence*). At this time, certain Christian communities were becoming politically vocal and far more active in the media, leading to the peculiar rise of televangelism. Its main proponent, Jimmy Swaggart, was frantically exposing the sexual indiscretions of rival ministers, whilst simultaneously being implicated in one of his own. It was a topic aching to be drawn upon, and the play, entitled *Carnage, A Comedy* premiered in 1987. It proved so popular that in 1988 it was already opening in the prestigious Tiffany Theatre on Sunset Boulevard, and by 1989, travelling to the Edinburgh Fringe Festival. It was for this leg that Black became a cast member, once again alongside Kyle Gass.

The Fringe Festival is renowned as the world's largest arts festival, a veritable melting pot of drama, comedy, music and dance; for three weeks every August, the city is taken over in the name of performing arts. What's more, there is no selection or vetting procedure, so it has a reputation for pioneering as many visionary acts as it does sub-standard ones. Anarchic, innovative and vital, it was the ideal place for The Actors' Gang to perform.

The time in Edinburgh brought Gass and Black together; they remember it as a case of 'if you can't beat 'em, join 'em' and, as Gass says, "I couldn't beat him." Kyle initially took a mentor role, taking Jack under his wing in an alliance that allowed his pride to remain unharmed. However, this dynamic did not prove particularly stable. "He looked up to me for about a day and a half!" Gass remarked in *Playboy*, "then realised I was full of shit and completely took over and dominated me after that." The run of *Carnage, A Comedy* was a huge success, remembered by many as one of the highpoints amongst the numerous Actors' Gang achievements. Indeed, in 2008 *Carnage* was reprised for the 25th Anniversary of The Actors' Gang, with Tim Robbins once again directing the production (this time without Black and Gass).

Back in the late 1980s, that initial run of the play also introduced Jack to the sharp sting and subsequent bitterness of a bad review. After the Edinburgh slot, the Gang took the production to the Public Theatre in New York, where Jack remembers an exceptionally successful performance: "We totally kicked its ass!" He stayed up all night, knowing that a reporter from the *New York Times* had been in the audience and the review would be published the next day. However, it was not as he expected; upon reading the review in the morning, he had to start laughing. The reporter, Black believes, seemed to almost bear a grudge against Robbins, and the review "could not have cut into [the play] more deeply." While Black asserts that the review was so bad it went beyond even being offensive, it was all the same a crushing disappointment – and one that, despite all Black's and Robbins' subsequent successes, they both still remember.

Upon returning from New York, Kyle Gass' college girlfriend ended their relationship, and he went into what Black remembers as somewhat of a personal crisis. Quitting the gang, Black immediately liked him more, regarding this new vulnerability as a counterpoint to his "tendency to be an a-hole"; perhaps he was also drawn in by the loner image that Gass had adopted. The bond was further galvanised when Jack's girlfriend at the time left him for her poetry teacher: "Pain and exile brought us together!" Bored and lonely, the two began hanging out all the more, and while they wouldn't have chosen to be so unceremoniously dumped, it was the genesis of a collaboration that would take them very far indeed.

Jack Black was acutely musical but despite being an accomplished singer, he was unable to play any instruments. He was eager to learn the guitar; while his utter failure in high school to cover 'Iron Man' convincingly had crushed his musical aspirations, his success in the Gang and his subsequent friendship with Gass had resurrected that dream. A deal was soon struck. Gass would give Jack lifetime guitar lessons in exchange for $200 and some help improving his acting. Gass was broke, single and bored – it seemed like a great way to make a bit of cash. And while he maintains that Jack was a quick learner, it required far more patience and work than he had initially anticipated. He remembers it as a painful process, having to endure a prolonged period where Black would simply strum the same three chords over and over. "You don't want to squelch his inspiration," he says, "but goddammit, it drove me insane." Jack recalls it in much the same way, reporting that he simply played the D, A and G chords over and over again. Fortunately, Gass had the good sense to apply Jack's minimal knowledge at this stage to a constructive framework, and introduced him to the beautifully simple progressions of rock 'n' roller Tom Petty. The first song Jack ever learnt was 'Runnin' Down A Dream', a single from Petty's 1989 album *Full Moon Fever* – though Gass remembers it only by reference to the lyrics: "The rain was unstoppable. That one." Building on this triumph, by the end of the first week, Black could play a whole set of Petty songs. Looking back, he knows he got a good deal from Gass. Despite not getting a lifetime of lessons, he is sure to have got far more than $200 worth, and feels guilty for subjecting Gass to the barrage of Petty. "I think guitar lessons are the most tedious thing on the planet," he remarked in *The Independent On Sunday*. "You have to have patience for someone playing the same three chords for three hundred hours." So what exactly, other than the pop-rock sensibilities of Tom Petty, drew them closer during this emotionally tumultuous period? First and foremost, it was the chemistry they shared. Black said on *www.joblo.com* that it quickly became obvious that the two had a connection: "It was like, you know, peanut butter and chocolate, lightning and thunder … When we're together, we are ten times the rock beast that we are alone. We're not just twice as powerful when we're together, but ten times as powerful. Like a transformer, a rock transformer." Secondly, Gass knew that they were sizing one another up for a possible song-writing collaboration. "We had already sniffed each other out as possible musical cohorts," he explains, and Jack had even played Gass a song he had written about his ex-girlfriend's betrayal. Gass greatly admired Black's vocal ability, and Jack already regarded Kyle as a "virtuoso" on the guitar. Finally, as Black reveals, they were encouraged by other, somewhat less artistic, external factors: "We smoked a lot of weed! I'll tell you that now."

Tenacious D did not yet exist, but all of the key elements were in place.

Chapter 3

TV MOVIES, METALLICA AND THE GENESIS OF TENACIOUS D

Jack had now been studying at UCLA for two years, spending much of his time working with Robbins and the Actor's Gang. Despite his success, Jack had decided there was no need for him to continue his academic studies. Gass had graduated six years prior, and feeling that it was no longer offering him what he wanted, in 1991 he dropped out. It was only his sophomore year at UCLA, but he was resolved to throw himself lock, stock and barrel into the entertainment industry. He moved back in with his mother in Culver City, and set about auditioning for TV shows and films.

He soon landed a role in the TV movie *Our Shining Moment*, which aired on June 2, 1991. He starred as an unnamed teenage hockey player, alongside Seth Green (who would later appear in the *Austin Powers* trilogy as Scotty) and Cindy Pickett (who has since become a successful TV actress). Written by Patrick

Hasburgh and funded in part by Walt Disney Television, it concerned a 1960s family, the father of whom had been laid off from work and decided to keep it secret from his family. After the man's thirteen-year-old son is expelled from school he encounters his father in the park in the middle of the day, and they agree to keep one another's secrets. However, no networks bought up the rights to the series, and it remained an unsold pilot.

After this initial disappointment, Jack was to land his feature film debut – and who else was to offer it him but Tim Robbins. On December 13, 1986, a short film had aired on legendary comedy show *Saturday Night Live* starring Robbins as a right-wing folk singer and anti-smoking lobbyist named Bob Roberts. The character had been developed over many years, first occurring to Robbins when he returned to the liberal Greenwich Village of New York, the area where he had been brought up, after an eight-year absence: "A lot of the artists and bohemian iconoclasts had just drifted away," he explained to Chris Roberge in *Interview*. "I noticed a lot of franchises opening up. I started thinking about what would happen if all of these businessmen picked up guitars. So I wrote him [Bob Roberts] as a businessman folk singer, and as the 1980s came his ambition grew, and by the 1990s he was running for office."

Since that first appearance on *Saturday Night Live*, Robbins had been developing a script for a feature based on this character, and had been passing it around various studios and production companies. Perhaps due to the film's heavy satirizing of the American right, or perhaps simply due to lack of foresight, it was ultimately the English production company Working Title who came up with the $4 million necessary to get the film made. 1992 had already been a successful year for Robbins – he had won the Best Actor Award at Cannes Film Festival for his starring role as Griffin Mill in Robert Altman's *The Player*. His good form continued when on September 4, 1992, *Bob Roberts* opened on general release.

Shot in a mockumentary style, the movie is essentially the chronicling of the title character's success as a politically motivated folk singer, and his attempt to win a senatorial campaign for the state of Pennsylvania. Robbins stars as Roberts himself, exuding all the remorseless self-aggrandising necessary to make his character despicable, enigmatic and magnetic in equal measure. He sneers, hoodwinks and gulls his way through the political arena, beating down his opponent (ably depicted by writer and real-life political candidate Gore Vidal) and building himself up. Brilliantly interwoven with the main thread of the film are a number of 'stock' footages of Roberts' musical endeavours, many of which Black took the opportunity to sing backing vocals on. Drawing heavily on the works of Bob Dylan, and in acute juxtaposition to Dylan's progressive attitudes, we are treated to the promos for 'The Times Are Changing Back', 'Wall Street Rap' and 'Drugs Stink'. Interestingly, despite the high quality of both satire and melody on offer here, Robbins refused to release a soundtrack album, fearing the neo-Conservative content of the songs would lead to them being misused. "I think that in the context of the film, they work, they're funny, and they're entertaining," he noted to *Interview*. "Out of context, I don't trust the songs. And I personally don't want to be driving in my car five years from now and hear that bile on the radio." The film also capably manipulates many of the scenes from *Don't Look Back,* the now legendary documentary shot by D. A. Pennebaker that chronicled Bob Dylan's 1965 UK tour – Robert's promo for 'Wall Street Rap', for example, is a razor sharp pastiche of the famous 'Subterranean Homesick Blues' clip that opens *Don't Look Back*. We are even treated to a homage to *This Is Spinal Tap,* whereby Roberts gets lost in a venue when he is due to perform on stage; Robbins states that Rob Reiner's 1984 classic was a big influence on the film, and this scene serves as his tip of the cap.

For all its artful internalisation of pop culture, the most admirable aspect of *Bob Roberts* is its level-headedness. It manages to use humour to highlight the shortcomings of the US political system, and those that move within it, without ever resorting to a partisan, party-political stance. It never becomes dry, transparent or didactic. We see both candidates in the senatorial race as essentially unsuitable for the responsibility they desire, and while we are left to assume Roberts is a Republican, the main weight of the film's condemnatory force falls upon the media. Robbins reflects that it is the superficiality of this vital sector that invites such unabashed criticism. This was partly inspired by an encounter Robbins had with a TV network anchor, when he asked why no stories were being ran about the controversial Iran Contra affair. "He said, 'Well, to do that we'd have to do a very in-depth piece, and people will turn their televisions off,'" he continued in *Interview*. "And what this taught me was that they have really entered into journalism as entertainment." *Bob Roberts* presents this dichotomy as an abdication of responsibility, a dereliction of duty, and a failing tantamount to negligence.

In the film, Black stars as one of Roberts' most devoted advocates, a dedicated disciple named Roger Davies who performs in a Roberts tribute group and zealously defends his name. It's a small part, but Black makes a big impact on the movie; staring unflinchingly at his hero through a window in the last act of the film, he deftly embodies the near-fanatical veneration that such uncompromising figures as Roberts are capable of attracting. Robbins even mentions Black on the DVD commentary following his first on screen appearance: "Jack ... really has a fervour in his eyes that I find so compelling and frightening. It's kind of this strange, sexual Nazi kind of weirdness, the psychopathic eyes of the truly devoted." But Black maintains that the part was not particularly challenging for him to play, as it wasn't a huge stretch from the reality of the situation. He recalls his absolute desperation to get the role: "I was dying for Tim Robbins to fucking accept me into his world and make me a mini-Tim Robbins," he said in *GQ*. "And the part was me just dying to be accepted into Bob Roberts' world and be a mini-Bob Roberts."

The film was well received by critics, who praised the judicious, intelligent tone that nonetheless maintained its humour and determination to entertain. However, it did seem to fall somewhat in the middle ground. For a few, the message was not driven home far enough; influential movie critic Roger Ebert, for example, asserted on www.rogerebert.suntimes.com that "if it had only been about campaign tactics and techniques, I would have liked it all the more." Some felt that that film sacrificed a degree of its weightiness in what was perceived as the flippancy of the depiction, but Robbins disagrees. 'I personally put a lot of pressure on myself to make this an entertaining film," he said at the time of its release, "and if it raises some questions, great … I hear reports from the lobbies of theatres about discussions and arguments. This is healthy." *Bob Roberts* performed modestly at the box office, grossing just under $4.5 million domestically. Again, Robbins was neither surprised nor concerned. He maintained that Hollywood regards political films as non-starters that simply wouldn't perform at the box office. "We'll see," he remarked. "I think that's hard to do."

Right now, Jack felt as if he had truly broken into the industry club that he dreamed about in his youth. He managed to get himself to the film's premier at the Cannes Film Festival, despite not having been invited – his father had recently moved there with his new wife, and it was a perfect pretence to slip away and rub shoulders with fellow movie stars. He truly felt as if his career had taken off, and now that he had impressed in a highly regarded film by a first time director, the offers were bound to come flooding in. He even managed to get to a party that director Robert Altman was throwing in his house in the hills above Cannes – Robbins had played the lead in Altman's latest film, *The Player* – to complete the Hollywood fantasy. He remembers it as a dream-like sequence, where he got the opportunity to smoke a joint with some major Hollywood players. "It doesn't get much more stony glamorous," Jack said. "I remember thinking, 'This is the beginning.'"

Unfortunately, it was actually only the beginning of a very slow period for Black. A string of TV parts followed, and while they helped to garner exposure and boost his CV, they seemed like a huge step down from the credibility of *Bob Roberts*. At the end of 1992 he would appear in *The Golden Palace*, the series that followed the hugely successful American sitcom *The Golden Girls,* as a taxi driver. However, the *Golden Palace* failed to match the popularity of its forerunner and lasted only one season. In January 1993, he appeared in *Marked for Murder*, a TV action movie directed by Mimi Leder. She would go on to direct, amongst other things, 1998's blockbuster disaster-movie *Deep Impact*, but Jack had little chance to make an impression with his bit part as a car thief. A few months later he appeared in another TV show, family drama *Life Goes On*, surprisingly as a skinhead.

Although momentum had stumbled, Jack had secured some more minor movie parts. The Quentin Tarantino penned *True Romance*, directed by Tony Scott, was due for release in September of the same year, and while he only had a tiny role as a movie attendant, it was to mark his second appearance on the silver screen. However, disastrously it soon transpired that his appearance had been cut from the final edit, and he missed his chance to be credited alongside such legendary figures as Gary Oldman, Brad Pitt, Samuel L. Jackson, Christopher Walken, and Dennis Hopper – not to mention the host of other performers who made up the incredible roll call of *True Romance* (while he didn't know it at the time, he would get some recompense, later having the opportunity to star alongside Walken and Hopper in more substantial roles). It was also not the last time he would be under the direction of Tony Scott, and on the next occasion, he would manage to keep himself in the picture. For the time being though, it was a set back he had not anticipated.

Fortunately, he had another movie role on release just one week after, though the credentials of the film were not quite so impressive. The Warner Brothers' *Airborne* is the story of Mitchell, a free-spirited Californian surfer who is forced to move to the mid-West when his parents relocate. Sneered at for his west coast, sun-kissed, floppy-fringed approach to life, he is forced to fall back on his formidable rollerblading skills to win the respect of his peers. The film gleefully plunders every exile-to-acceptance cliché you might dare to mention, from heavy-browed bullies to geeky cousins to off-limits love interests, and even climaxes in a triumphant rollerblading race across 'the Devil's Backbone'. In time honoured fashion, enemies shake hands, boys and girls kiss, and everyone learns a lesson.

Black puts in a good turn as Augie, one of a trio of hockey playing hoodlums who resolve to make Mitchell's life more difficult. He's clearly too old for the sixteen or seventeen he's supposed to be, but his trademark arching brows belie a malevolence befitting of the role, and he brings a charming goofiness to the otherwise plain part. He's at his most recognisable when firing off at Mitchell, displaying the trademark hair-trigger temper that has become such a recognisable element of his performances, and the opportunity to flex his comic muscles once again must have proved too tempting to resist. It also gave him the chance to star alongside Seth Green in earnest, who played Mitchell's cousin Wiley; he had also worked on *Our Shining Moment.*

The movie did not fare well with critics, however, with most agreeing that while it might entertain younger children, adolescents would find the scrupulous adherence to formula most uninspiring; Jack's performance, too, went largely unnoticed. The film failed to fill many seats, just managing to clear its estimated $2.6 million budget. It wasn't exactly a rousing success for Black, or even the best role he'd had – but it was the largest, and he did, at least, end 1992 moving in the right direction ... albeit slowly.

1993, however, went much slower. It was a period of his life that he recalls with some disdain, being forced to go back and live at his mum's house and find small scraps of work to keep himself afloat – "just hoping, waiting, trying." He would have to wait until October to see himself in any work at all, in Season 5 of *Northern Exposure*, a drama/comedy set in the remote Alaskan town of Cicely. He starred as Kevin Wilkins, one of only three students graduating from the tiny high school. Later in October he would appear in the sci-fi blockbuster *Demolition Man*, helpfully credited as 'Wasteland Scraps'. In a blink-and-you'll-miss-it moment, he is seen flinching as Sylvester Stallone waves a gun around at him and his cohorts. Jack, however, can't quite remember if he's in the movie at all, claiming that he's pretty sure you can't even see him in the final cut. He also remembers diligently turning up every day to perform his meagre role as an extra, and waiting for the one day that he was going to be prominently featured on camera. Unfortunately for him, when that day came around he overslept, and it was a blunder that didn't go unnoticed. "I remember the producer, Joel Silver, called my agent," he jokingly told James King of BBC Radio 1, "and he was so furious, he said, 'He better be dead!' It wasn't fair. I mean three months showing up every day, right on time, and then the day that I oversleep is the day that they decide is my close-up … But I showed him, I became famous. In your face, Joel Silver!"

Fortunately, upsetting one of the biggest producers in Hollywood didn't stop the work coming, and 1994 proved not only busy but also very productive. First Jack landed a role in another TV movie, HBO's *Blind Justice*; it follows a partially-sighted gunfighter as he attempts to protect a new-born baby, though this inevitably involves shooting some people up along the way. Black's role is small, appearing only briefly as an anonymous private, looking remarkably incongruous in light of his later roles. Next, he appeared in the TV series *Monty*, a sit-com concerning a conservative talk-show hosts wrangling with his decidedly more left-wing family. Jack appeared in a small speaking role as Doug, but the show was uninspired and flat, and the plug was pulled just a few episodes in. He also appeared in another Mimi Leder TV movie, the roundly panned *The Innocent*. It starred Kelsey Grammar (who had at the time appeared in just one season of *Frasier* as Dr. Crane) as a detective, determined to protect an autistic boy who is the key witness in a murder. Black had another bit part as Marty Prago.

Jack's acting career was ticking over nicely, but he still made sure he found time to spend with Gass. Now a competent guitarist himself, he had began incubating the idea of a possible act, based on the duo's acerbic banter and grand ambitions. Black still remembered the humiliation of his high school musical debut (where he had abandoned the performance of Black Sabbath's 'Iron Man' midway due to the utter disinterest of the audience), but the dynamic he and Gass shared had set him thinking: *what if they were to play music – earnestly, and skilfully – but with a twist?*

Prior to meeting Jack, Gass' musical tastes had been decidedly more mellow. He inclined towards the softer end of guitar music, citing James Taylor and Crosby, Stills and Nash as two abiding influences. This was something Jack appreciated but, in Gass' words, "he considered me a softy." Jack was now determined to steel Gass to some more abrasive sounds, and he set about force-feeding his companion on a comprehensive diet of rock's most prominent acts. One of the key elements of this unholy mission were heavy metal godfathers Metallica and their magnum opus, 'One', has its own special place in the Tenacious D saga. The track itself, taken from 1988's *...And Justice For All,* is near-legendary: based on Dalton Trumbo's novel *Johnny Got His Gun*, it operates as the monologue of a solider who has lost all four limbs, as well as his sight, speech and hearing. Over the course of its seven-minute running time, it shifts from glassy, melodic instrumentals to taut power-chord riffery, finally climaxing in an intense machine-gun barrage of noise. The accompanying music video, as their first ever, drew heavy criticism from die-hard fans – nonetheless, the song earned Metallica a Grammy for 'Best Metal Performance' in 1990.

It was around four years later that Jack Black was trying to convince his friend Kyle Gass that 'One' was, in fact, the greatest song ever written, by the best band in the world. Kyle was not immediately convinced. "He listened to it thrice," Jack recalled on www.joblo.com. "At first he said nay. Then he said perhaps. And then he said yeah." On further consideration, however, Jack was forced to qualify that *every* song Metallica wrote was in fact the greatest song ever, due to the epic, grandiose intent of the writing. And it was this realisation, claims Black, that truly engendered Tenacious D. As two awe-inspired fans, armed only with acoustic guitars, there was the potential for a truly original and funny act. The idea also appealed to Kyle. "As fledging songwriters," he also noted, "it doesn't cost anything to try and write the greatest song ever." However, the idea developed after this initial conception, most likely affected by the admission that writing the greatest song ever is no mean feat. Jack came up with the ideal solution – to not write the greatest song ever, but a *tribute* to it. Initially, Kyle was baffled, admitting that he didn't have a clue what Black had in mind. But he soon caught on, and the two penned their first (and arguably their most famous) song: 'Tribute'.

Armed with this single song, the as-yet-unnamed duo set about securing their first live performance. Soon enough they were booked to support Abe Lincoln Story, a self-proclaimed "soul-punk-swing" band the duo knew from the LA scene (Abe Lincoln Story had previously toured with Weezer, as would Tenacious D later in their career). The venue was Al's Bar in Downtown LA, a hotspot for up-and-coming music and comedy acts. However, these were hard times for comedy. Black recalls the pressure that many at the time felt to move on from stand-up, with the typical "did-you-ever-notice?" patter of observational comedy becoming worn and overused. But the lynchpin of Tenacious D, even at this early stage, was firmly in place: two gawky, awkward, overweight men with aspirations of being rock superstars, equipped only with acoustic guitars and Black's flamboyant vocal styling. But the interaction between self-perception and reality was – and is – more complex than this. They might have only had one song, but it was genuinely *good*. Black could really sing and Gass could really play the guitar. On top of this central contradiction, the lyrics were sharply self-referential, a habit Black claims he learnt from Jon Spencer (the enigmatic front man of New York punk trio the Jon Spencer Blues Explosion). "[Spencer] was a huge influence on me, specifically the shameless self-referencing," he told *Blender*. "That was a huge influence on Tenacious D. A kind of hypnosis takes place: If you keep saying you're the best, some people are going to believe it. It's manipulative, but if it's funny, it's excusable."

It is surely no coincidence that the same year Gass and Black played their first gig, The Jon Spencer Blues Explosion had released *Orange* on Matador records, an album Black frequently cites as one of his favourites. Clearly, the shameless self-referencing *was* funny. On the night of the debut gig, there were a large number of alternative comedians in the audience, Jack recalls, and they weren't going to be entertained, still less laugh, at overused jokes. "You had to shock them and do something really different," he says. "I don't want to toot our own horns, but what we were doing bordered on performance art." And while it might not have registered with the audience that they were witnessing art, reports state that they found it very amusing. "We played our one song," said Black in *The East Bay Express*, "and I'm sure I'm exaggerating this in my mind, but I remember the audience kind of flipping out. They were cheering very hard. There were screams, laughter, and a very big supportive ovation. Might've even been a couple of tears." With only one song, it wasn't just the music that kept the laughs rolling in. The on-stage banter was present right from this first performance, a fact which Gass attributes to it being so organic to how the pair relate. Black played the hawkish egomaniac, demanding absolute dedication from Gass' unassuming fall-guy; though Kyle does note that "Jack seems like he's always a little meaner to me on stage."

The enthusiastic reaction was one Gass was not expecting – he remembers feeling physically sick with the pressure of the situation. He had never been in a band before meeting Jack and his only live performances as a musician had been in the pit, providing the music for Actors' Gang productions. He couldn't fathom why the audience were responding so positively, and yet, they were. This wasn't the only unusual aspect of the gig; it also contained an element of audience participation quite unlike anything you would ordinarily expect to witness. The crowd had the opportunity to name the band.

There were four options: 'Pets or Meat', 'Balboa's Biblical Theatre', 'The Axe Lords featuring Gorgazon's Mischief', and

'Tenacious D'. Gass' personal favourite was 'The Axe Lords...', but as a unit, the pair had decided Tenacious D was the most appropriate. With this in mind, they provided this option last, knowing it would probably garner the most votes. Unfortunately, it didn't. But no one could ever accuse Gass and Black of taking themselves too seriously: opting for benevolent dictatorship over democracy, they gave their loyal subjects the finger and forced Tenacious D through anyway. It was a phrase they had picked up from basketball announcer Marv Albert, who would often refer to the sound defending of a given team as 'tenacious', crying, "That's some tenacious D!" Speaking to *Esquire* magazine in 2003, Gass and Black saw fit to mystify this aspect of their history and deny the claims that this is where their moniker had originated from. "It's just not true!" Black exclaimed, though Gass added, "it's good that people have bought into the Marv Albert campaign of misinformation. One day the truth will be revealed." This is in stark contrast to Black's comments just five months earlier, when he name-checked Marv Albert to a British reporter on www.virtualfestivals.com. He also said, perhaps fearing a sense of exclusion on British fans' part, "I'm sure people can play tenacious defence in rugby or cricket or any of your local sports. Defence my friend. It's the key to winning." (Perhaps the comments to *Esquire* had something to do with the forthcoming 2006 Tenacious D film they were promoting. "The reason I can't tell you right now is because it's a central plot point in the upcoming Tenacious D movie," he helpfully revealed. The film contains no mention of how the pair got their name.)

But back in 1994, long before a film, an album or even a single were feasible, that first gig was notable for more than just rabid crowd response and the coronation of Tenacious D as rock contenders. There were also two particular people in the audience that day that are deserving of a mention. The first is Harry Shearer, the American actor who brilliantly portrayed vacuous bassist Derek Smalls in *This Is Spinal Tap*. The film that effectively launched the mockumentary as a distinct genre (though examples existed prior to this), *Spinal Tap* chronicled the rise and fall and rise again of the film's titular hapless hard rockers. Hilariously lampooning the self-aggrandising character of rock music and its exponents, revealing its pomposity and ridiculousness but with a real sense of affection, it was a film that Tenacious D doubtlessly drew from in the creation of their on-stage personas. The key difference is that while Spinal Tap were presented as a jaded band facing a down-turn in their popularity, Tenacious D have always played the part of the ambitious newcomers, desperate to impress and brimming with enthusiasm. Shearer (who would also later voice characters such as Mr. Burns, Smithers, Ned Flanders and Seymour Skinner in *The Simpsons*) was a regular at Al's Bar, but his appearance at the gig carries a symbolic resonance too profound to resist. Shearer was sizing Tenacious D up for the mock-rock crown; and given the wholehearted embrace that their performance received, one imagines he discovered they were the perfect fit.

The other guest of honour was also a regular customer, the American comedian David Cross. Cross had become well known on the alternative comedy scene, cutting his teeth amongst many other comics in New York's 'Catch a Rising Star' club, famous for hosting fledgling performances from comedy luminaries such as Andy Kaufman and Larry David. He had since written on *The Ben Stiller Show*, a short-running but well received Fox series that launched the career of Stiller and fellow comedian Andy Dick. It was also the first major appearance of co-creator Judd Apatow – who has since scored hits with the likes of *The 40 Year-Old Virgin, Knocked Up* and *Superbad*. In 1994 David Cross was already developing a new TV show, and impressed by the performance he witnessed, he introduced himself to the band. Black remembers the conviction in their act that the first gig had given to them, and the D launched into what he refers to as an "overconfident spree of gigs." Cross was vital in facilitating this process, introducing the band to the alternative comedy scene in LA and its hotspots. Tenacious D were soon performing at clubs such as Largo, HBO Workspace and UnCabaret, where Cross had made his LA stand-up debut, and they quickly garnered a reputation as a must-see act. However, it is important to remember that at this stage the pair remained a comedy duo and no more; while they impressed with the quality of their songs, they were still essentially just affecting the pose of rock stars, not yet feeling confident enough to play regular music venues. "We're not very confident performers, and if we don't get a laugh we get insecure," Gass said to Neil Strauss of *The New York Times* at the time. "If we got the regular rock gigs, we'd be a failure. We feel more comfortable rocking a comedy room as opposed to laughing it up with a rock crowd. I'd love to do the straight music thing, but that's kind of against our mission, which is to rebel against the serious singer-songwriter mentality." At this stage, the idea of headline slots and platinum albums was clearly a million miles from what Jack and Kyle expected.

With Tenacious D's auspicious beginning behind him, Black finished out the year with one last movie role, this time in *The Neverending Story III*. Much like his role in *Airborne*, he played a bully with an improbable name (Slip); though this time his dullard's affability was replaced with sheer malice. Clad in a leather biker jacket and shaven-headed, he pursues the hero with The Nasties, a gang of goth-misfit-sycophants. While Black did his best to inject some vigour into the role, it was character-type writing at its most reductive and there was very little to work with. The film ran over-schedule and arrived late in cinemas, receiving only a very limited release. And despite its being called *The Neverending Story*, the writers had in fact ran out of source material – the 1979 book that was the basis of the films had, by the close of the second film, ended. The third instalment is often regarded as an unwelcome bolt-on by fans, and Jack was once again to suffer the disappointment of an underperforming film. However, he has been known to claim that *The Neverending Story III* is the most worth renting of his early films. Not that he believes it to be a good performance: "It's definitely the funniest ... just because of how bad it is."

Chapter 4

JACK'S SEARCH FOR INSPIRADO

1995 began in much the same way as 1994; that is, with TV work. Jack was first cast in an episode of *All American Girl*, an ABC sitcom about a Korean-American woman and her quarrelsome family. Jack's new cohort David Cross was also to star in the show, as would Quentin Tarantino for a *Pulp Fiction* parody; but the relationship between stand-up comic/star Margaret Cho and the network was contentious. The tone and style constantly shifted throughout the series, and as such, it was cancelled after just one season. After *All American Girl* came another sitcom for Jack, an episode of *Pride And Joy*, where he starred as an unnamed character. This time the show failed to even see out a full season. Jack must have been beginning to think he was cursed. Fortunately, he soon scored another movie role, in the comedy/drama *Bye Bye Love*. Its most notable star was Randy Quaid, as one of a trio of middle-aged divorcees, though Black appears only briefly as a DJ at a party. The film was only a modest success at the box office.

Jack then moved on to what has become one of the most maligned films in recent memory – Kevin Reynolds' *Waterworld*. It is set in a post-apocalyptic future where the polar ice caps have melted, causing the surface of the Earth to be entirely covered in water. Kevin Costner, who also produced the picture, plays a man known only as the Mariner, born with gills and webbed feet so as to be better adapted to the new environment. Over the course of the film, he is forced into protecting a young girl and her guardian, believing that the young girl holds the key to finding dry land. While this may sound like a premise Black would delight in – it isn't a million miles from the films that he relished in his youth – the film was beset with problems and almost written off before it was released. The budget spiralled out of control, with final estimates resting somewhere around the $175 million mark, thus bestowing it with the (dubious) honour of being the most expensive film ever made (until *Titanic* two years later). There were even various rumours about director Reynolds leaving the project and discontinuing his association with the film, which Costner then worked on himself. However, Reynolds remains credited as sole director. Ironically, while *Waterworld* didn't exactly set the box office alight, in ultimately produced a healthy return on Universal's massive investment, perhaps due in part to the controversy that surrounded it.

Black appears as a pilot, barley recognisable under a flying cap, goggles and a layer of grease as he leers out of his bi-plane. Despite the brevity of his on-screen appearance, it was his opportunity to right a wrong and finally be credited alongside Dennis Hopper; a distinction he'd missed out on after being cut from *True Romance*.

After years of knocking on the door of primetime TV and receiving only bit parts in response, Jack finally got a sizeable role in one of the most popular shows of the 1990s; *The X-Files* (this popular and long-running sci-fi series followed the investigations of FBI agents Fox Moulder and Dana Scully into all things extraterrestrial and supernatural). He starred in the episode 'D. P. O.' alongside Giovanni Ribisi, who would also move on to bigger and better things – not least a role in Spielberg's *Saving Private Ryan*. Black starred as Bart 'Zero' Liquori, the best friend of Ribisi's Darren Peter Oswald who has taken on the ability to channel electricity through his person. However, it soon emerges that he's not been particularly discreet about his talents, and Mulder and Scully are called in to investigate a number of electricity-related deaths. Jack excels as Zero, and had grown his hair down to his shoulders for the part. A slacker employee of the local arcade and conscientious objector of Darren's murderous ways, he informs Mulder and Scully of Oswald's power and is subsequently murdered himself. It was a great part for Black, one which boosted his exposure in TV and gave him a chance to stretch his legs a little more. And according to the man himself, the were other perks to the job. "I'm pretty sure I could've gotten some off of [Gillian] Anderson," he cheekily joked on EW.com. "I mean, she never said anything but there was some eye contact where it was like, 'Whoah…' And I was like, 'C'mon, let's keep this professional. We got a job to do." He certainly wasn't intimidated by David Duchovny either, the actor who played Fox Mulder. In fact, he asserts that he outshone him: "I took him to the hole, slammed in his face. Acting dunk."

In October and November, three more TV shows aired featuring the prolific Jack Black; the first two being *Touched By An Angel* and *The Single Guy*, respectively. *Touched By An Angel* follows a group of angels as they go about their divinely ordained business (he starred in the episode 'Angels On The Air'). *The Single Guy* was a series that managed to shoehorn every sitcom convention into its two season run, and was one of a glut of shows that flooded the market after the monumental success of *Seinfeld*. Black starred as Randy in the Season One episode 'Sister'. The third TV show, however, is one far more memorable for Black's performance. As explained, since witnessing their debut gig at Al's Bar, writer and stand-up comedian David Cross had taken a notable interest in Tenacious D and had subsequently been instrumental in introducing the pair to LA's alternative comedy circuit. But he had also been in pre-production for a new show with his friend and collaborator Bob Odendirk; and when the series was commissioned by HBO, he asked Jack to feature. It was entitled *Mr. Show With Bob And David*, and while initial ratings were modest, it quickly became a cult hit. It was a brilliantly absurd and eccentric sketch show, combining live and pre-recorded skits and often featuring musical numbers. Its chorus of oddball characters ape much of Monty Python, as does its convention of linking all the sketches together, even if by the most tenuous thread. However, it was a distinctly modern, American creation, with a bold counter-culture streak; the show's various writers delighted in sending up the cult of celebrity, pop culture and consumer gullibility for ridicule. Black was to appear in two episodes of the first season, the most memorable being his appearance in the second show, 'What to Think', where he had the chance to demonstrate not only his talent as a comedian, but also his distinctive singing voice. In the sketch 'The Joke: The Musical', a loose *Rocky Horror Picture Show* parody, a travelling leather pant salesman is forced to approach a local farmhouse for help when his car breaks down. Black appears, clad in a straw hat and dungarees, agreeing to let the salesman sleep in his barn. He warns, however, of one condition; the three holes the salesman sees in the wall are "not for thee," and prancing playfully around the stage, he launches into a rousing chorus of "don't stick your dick in these holes." However, as the salesmen falls asleep, Black reappears, this time dressed as Satan. He implores the man to stop being so weak, and even employs his distinctive arm-flapping trot in the temptation; a move that has become a staple of his stage and screen antics. Finally, the man succumbs, and finding the first two holes to his liking, moves on to the third, only to be gripped and held until morning. At this point, the farmer reappears, and reveals that the first two holes were his daughter and wife; but the third was his milking machine, which does not stop milking until fifty gallons are withdrawn. The sketch ends with the salesman freeing himself, and Odendirk appearing dressed as the milking machine to sing a song of his woe. It is Black, however, who steals the sketch, his energy and physicality eclipsing the other performers. It was a key appearance – for the first time he was able to bring the larger-than-life charisma of his Tenacious D persona to the TV screen.

But the highlight of the year was to come at the end. While these filler roles might have put money in his pocket, in July of 1995 Black had wrapped on another Tim Robbins project that was due for release in December, and he was desperately eager to see how it had turned out. It was called *Dead Man Walking* and is the story of a convicted murderer named Matt Poncelet, played by Sean Penn, who presides on death row. With his execution impending, he is befriended by a nun, who battles to have his appeal heard and simultaneously invites the disdain and ire of those around her.

Jack remembers his time with Sean Penn, an actor he greatly admired, as intimidating and somewhat unsettling; he notes that to match his incredible talent he harboured a disconcerting intensity. He recalls his behaviour off-screen as erratic and unpredictable. "He would burst into spontaneous psychobabble poetry and the whole room would go silent and uncomfortable," said Jack. "No one would know what to say next ... Not a fun hang." That said, he maintains that his performance on screen justifies his antics off. "It was like, 'Holy crap. This guy is on another planet – he's on Planet Fucking Great Super Acting.'"

And Fucking Great Super Acting it most certainly was. It earned Penn an Oscar nomination, which he unforgivably lost to Nicholas Cage for *Leaving Las Vegas.* Penn does indeed bring an incredible intensity to the role, one that constantly threatens to explode into paroxysms of rage, while on the exterior he remains detached and calculating. Over the course of the film he superbly modulates toward vulnerability, exposing his humanity more and more, and subsequently becoming more dignified in his conduct. Robbin's wife Susan Sarandon plays Helen Prejean, the nun who befriends Poncelet – and she rightly won a 'Best Actress Oscar'. In pitying Poncelet she never belittles; faced with the horror of his crime she never balks; and in desperately fighting for his redemption she neither devalues him nor overvalues herself. Prejean is shown to be confused and frightened, but all the same hopelessly drawn to help the man who has thrown himself at her mercy.

Black appears as Poncelet's brother, Craig. The family are allowed one last meeting before Poncelet is to be put to death, and while it lasts but a few minutes, it is a very important scene for the dynamic of the film. Robbins notes himself in the director's commentary that it humanises Poncelet, shows him to have a family who he loves, and brothers who look up to him. But the heartbreaking conclusion to the scene is that, before the end of the meeting, the family have nothing left to say; the burden of the pain is too great, they are entirely ill-equipped to express it, and so they mutely leave Poncelet to face his fate alone.

It is the story of a man dehumanised by both his guilt and the pariah status his actions have forced upon him. For this, Robbins deserves much credit. The film did well in smaller independent cinemas, and even saw some success in larger theatres, becoming a sleeper hit. It grossed almost $40 million in US alone, easily outstripping its $11 million budget.

With the success of *Dead Man Walking* and *The X-Files* having made Black a regular for small roles in big pictures, 1995 was effectively the end of his career as an extra. It's not a time he feels particularly affectionate about, but he maintains that all the years at the bottom did leave a marked impression on him, and that he always sympathises with the extras on set. "It's not an easy gig if you don't have any lines," he asserts. "You're just waiting around. It can be a sad, long journey."

The pace of his career was certainly starting to quicken and 1996 was a busy year indeed. He kicked it off with another TV appearance, over two episodes of *Picket Fences*, a CBS show about the bizarre occurrences in a small town. The rest of the year was given over to walk-on film roles, and he was cast in no less than five. The first was *Crossworlds,* a sci-fi film about a dimension-hopping college student and his attempts to save the universe.

Black starred as the stereotypical hero's roommate, helpfully described by one critic as a "frat house crushed under one shirt." The film had only a very limited release, and despite generally positive reviews, it failed to generate any real buzz. Next, Tenacious D were to appear on screen for the very first time, as their growing reputation in LA, and Jack's experience as an actor, had caught the attention of various figures within the industry. They appeared only briefly, in Jason Bloom's 1996 flop *Bio-dome*, a film which attracted an almost impressive degree of disdain from critics and movie-goers alike. It even managed to win star Pauly Shore a Razzie – a mock award singling out the worst in film – for 'Worst Actor'. Perhaps it was fortuitous, then, that the band are simply playing in the background during one scene, though Black and Gass do distinctly remember being on set. Despite the film's failure, Tenacious D's appearance was a clear indication that their star was in the ascent.

Next, Jack was cast in Ben Stiller's *The Cable Guy*, perhaps partly owing to David Cross' connection with Stiller (as mentioned Cross had written for his short-running TV show on Fox in 1992). It was the largest movie role Black had secured to date, and it also presented the opportunity to star alongside one of the decade's biggest comedy stars, Jim Carrey. Carrey was paid $20 million to star in the film, the highest single pay-check for an actor at the time. Black's memories of Carrey are perhaps slightly at odds with this monumental fee; he recalls that, during the filming of one scene, Carrey waited for action before unleashing an immense fart, and then began as if nothing had happened. This impressed Jack. "He doesn't give a shit what anyone thinks," he realised, "and that's why he's so funny."

The film saw Carrey cast in the eponymous role, a peculiar cable technician called Ernie "Chip" Douglas. After allowing a customer named Steve (played by Matthew Broderick) illegal access to all channels, the two become friends, but Chip becomes irrationally attached. Chip's behaviour becomes increasingly outlandish, however, and Steve attempts to distance himself; from here in, Chip becomes threatening. Jack plays Steve's friend Rick, who despite initially advising Steve to bribe Chip, is ultimately jostled out of the "best friend" spot. Irritated and jealous, Rick cuts off contact with Steve, until Chip's erratic conduct convinces him to help.

The film marked a radical departure for Carrey, who despite having made a career of playing madcap characters, was not previously cast in dark roles. This said, he makes decent work of it; the film is indeed somewhat unsettling, and while humour and trepidation can be uneasy bedfellows, Stiller deftly intertwines the two. Carrey hits all the right notes, seeming as vulnerable as he is intimidating, as funny as he is creepy. Broderick is almost in a supporting role, but he is suitably hapless as the object (or target) of Chip's affection. Black also impresses as Rick, comfortably fitting into the role of an irritably tempered but ultimately benevolent friend – though the role is somewhat restrictive in its breadth, and does not allow him to fully demonstrate the extent of his talent. Black's most memorable scene comes when the escalating rivalry between Chip and Rick is played out on a basketball court, the tension making for an aggressive, confrontational match. Played out in slow-motion, every grimace and snarl of Carrey's character becomes all the more telling, and we see for the first time the malevolent degree of his eccentricities. It climaxes in Chip clambering up Rick to make a slam dunk, which sends a shower of glass raining down over the other players. Rick sardonically quips, "Thanks for bringing your friend, Steven" – it's a strange reversal of expectation, in light of his later roles, to see Black bemused at another's weirdness. Nonetheless, it's one that works well, and Black even managed to secure a cameo for Kyle Gass – we see him watching TV and reaching for a beer toward the end of the story.

The film also functions as a clever indictment of TV dependency. The Cable Guy was essentially raised by TV, and his enemy, Rick, is a cameraman; we get a running commentary of the trial of two murderers from TV footage, but the signal compellingly cuts out before a verdict can be delivered; and the film's intense denouement is played out on a satellite dish. There were layers to the script that many viewers simply failed to pick up on. But with all this said, the film is ultimately somewhat strained. Toward the close everyone seems unsure as to whether the audience should be laughing or grimacing, and Chip's on-screen breakdown incites far more pity than laughter.

The disquieting effect of Carrey's performance proved too rich for many critics' palate, and the film received a decidedly mixed response. Roger Ebert perhaps best sums up the aftertaste that the film left in the mouths of many reviewers. The first line of his report reads, "We want to like Jim Carrey. A movie that makes us dislike him is a strategic mistake," and the last line reads, "Black comedy is not what you pay someone $20 million to do." While it didn't deserve the bashing it got from many corners of the media, it is too deeply flawed to be called a great film. All the same, despite popular mythology condemning it as a relative flop, it actually grossed over $100 million.

The Cable Guy is also significant for another reason – its credits saw Jack Black, Ben Stiller, Owen Wilson, Leslie Mann and Judd Apatow all listed together. And while *USA Today* had not yet coined the term, many see these collaborations on the film as the first emergence of the so-called 'Frat Pack', the group of actors who have come to dominate mainstream American comedy since the Millennium. Wilson and Black were only minor players at this stage, but they would come to be hugely significant in the perception and success of a certain group of actors, of whom they are at the fore. Stiller and Apatow, on the other hand, were already attracting a lot of attention as the potential torch-carriers of comedy into the new Millennium.

With *The Cable Guy* released in June, Black would have to wait five months for his next release: *The Fan*, starring Wesley Snipes and Robert De Niro. Coincidentally, the film also dealt with themes of obsession and instability, albeit in a far more straight-faced manner, and Jack once again played a TV station employee. His role is tiny, but he at least got the chance to actually appear in a Tony Scott film (having been completely cut from *True*

Romance), just as he was able to star alongside Dennis Hopper in *Waterworld*. It was not to be his last gig with De Niro, either.

November also saw the air-date of Episode 3 of *Mr Show*, which following its cult success, was now in its Second Season. Black's dual talents as an actor and singer were once again called into service, this time for a parody of Tim Rice and Andrew Lloyd Webber's rock opera, *Jesus Christ Superstar*. Entitled 'Jeepers Creepers Semi-Star', Black plays the title character who, in marked contrast to the actual Messiah, spends his time getting high and playing golf videogames. Frustrated by his follower's insistence he actually do something, he challenges their righteousness with a cry of "who will throw the first stone?" – to which, a rock is thrown at his head. Finally, his parents ask their slacker son to leave, and Jeepers implores, "Forgive them God! Or don't. It's entirely up to you." The sketch ends with Cross and Odendirk explaining that 'Jeepers Creepers Semi-star' was the biggest failure in Broadway history, opening and closing on the same night. Black also appeared briefly in the final episode of season two, in the sketch 'Coupon: the Movie', as a none-too impressed but nonetheless enthusiastic movie-goer.

Black closed out a successful 1996 with a solid role in Tim Burton's *Mars Attacks!* Based on a 1960s card trading series, it featured a fine and extensive ensemble cast, including Jack Nicholson (in two roles), Pierce Brosnan, Danny DeVito and Michael J. Fox. With hideous Martians invading the Earth, slaughtering its inhabitants and destroying the landscape, Black plays an incompetent, ill-educated soldier who volunteers to greet the alien visitors. Despite his willingness to honour his county, he is spectacularly killed in the first attack, fried to a glowing skeleton whilst still clutching an American flag. His family set up a shrine to him in their trailer, dubbing him an "American Hero," until their refusal to leave their home also sees them killed. While the majority of critics regarded it very poorly on release, Black's habit of starring in cult projects was kept alive when the film found a devoted fan base. It grossed over $100 million, comfortably clearing its $70 million budget.

★ ★ ★

Jack saw in the New Year of 1997 with Tenacious D, who having grown in reputation and confidence, had graduated to playing larger venues. In addition to this, they had finally found the self-belief to play not only comedy clubs, but dedicated music venues. In January they were doing a run of shows at The Viper Room, a nightclub on Sunset Strip, LA. At this time it was still part owned by Johnny Depp, and had become notorious in 1993 for the death of fellow actor River Phoenix by drug overdose; yet in 1997 it was still a hotspot for celebrity revellers. Tenacious D had been booked to play every Sunday for an indefinite time, operating as a house band of sorts, and the staff no doubt became pretty familiar with the D's shtick. One particular employee was to have a massive bearing on Tenacious D's development, though the duo had no idea at the time; his name was Pete Stahl. Prior to working at The Viper Room as a barman, he had been the vocalist in influential hardcore band Scream. As key exponents of the so-called D.C. sound, they were stalwarts of the Dischord Records label, established by Minor Threat front man Ian MacKaye. MacKaye would later go on to front Fugazi, a band that Black refers to as "the kings of integrity". "Whenever me or Kyle does something selfless, we always say that we're 'pullin' a Fugazi.'"

After Scream's third album, drummer Kent Stax left for personal reasons. The band held open auditions for a new drummer, and a seventeen-year-old Dave Grohl attended. He had been playing guitar for years, but had recently taught himself the rudiments of drumming – though he had to claim he was twenty in order to qualify for the audition. To his surprise, Scream asked him to join, and over the next four years he toured extensively and cut two LP's with the band. But following the sudden break-up of Scream in 1990, Grohl travelled to Seattle to see a band called Nirvana, who had recently recorded their debut *Bleach*. They too had been auditioning for a drummer, and having been impressed with Grohl's work in Scream, then asked him to join the band.

The rest of the story has duly been inducted into rock 'n' roll mythology. Nirvana's sophomore effort, *Nevermind,* was released on 24 September, 1991. With the heavy airplay of debut single 'Smells Like Teen Spirit', the band were catapulted to international fame, and *Nevermind* topped the *Billboard* album charts in January 1992. They re-wrote the standards of what an underground, alternative band could be expected to achieve, effectively bringing alternative rock to the mainstream and altering the sound of popular music forever. Front man Kurt Cobain quickly became a cult idol, with many drawn to the polarity of his diffidence in interviews and on-stage fervour, not to mention his intuitive song-writing ability. While third album *In Utero* failed to sell as well as *Nevermind,* it nonetheless topped the *Billboard* charts in September 1993. By April 1994, however, Cobain's heroin use had spiralled out of control and he was persuaded to check into rehab. He left the facility, returned home, and was found dead on April 8 from a self-inflicted gunshot.

Not surprisingly, Grohl initially became withdrawn after Cobain's unexpected death, but found that music offered him a degree of solace. In October he recorded fifteen demos, playing all the instruments himself and passed the demo around a few labels. He soon signed to Capitol Records, and not wanting to be perceived as a solo artist, released the album under the moniker *The Foo Fighters*. Interestingly, parallels between Black and Grohl were already emerging; in the interim between Cobain's death and the release of The Foo Fighters' debut, Grohl briefly drummed for Tom Petty and the Heartbreakers – the first artist that Black learnt to play on the guitar. Similarly, just four months after Black's appearance on *The X-Files*, Grohl would also make a cameo.

But it was during the recording of The Foo Fighters' second album that Tenacious D and Grohl's paths first crossed. After troubled sessions in Washington D.C., Grohl opted to move the band to the Grandmaster Recorders Studio in LA at the beginning of 1997. It was while working here that his former band-mate, Pete Stahl, got in touch to recommend going to see a gig by Tenacious D. Grohl remembers his initial reluctance to drag himself from the studio; "He [Stahl] said, 'You have to come see this band.' I bailed the first three Sundays and then he forced me to come down." The band had no idea Grohl was in attendance, but he decided to give the boys some encouragement before their performance, "just to turn up the heat a little and make sure there was something worth watching." Kyle remembers him coolly wishing them good luck "like he was just a nobody," though Jack says it certainly fired them up for the show: "I think it did give us a little goose. We cranked it up a couple of notches." It is not particularly remarkable that Black should want to impress Grohl – he had been a Nirvana fan since the release of *Bleach*, and while Grohl hadn't drummed on that album, it had left a lasting impression on Jack. The duo also remember their manager (perhaps understandably) trying to court Grohl for some help getting a deal. After the gig, Dave began talking to the band, only to be set upon: "Our manager was like, 'Okay, Tenacious D's here, you like 'em, you've got a record company…'" Dave didn't bite, and Jack claims he was so angry, "steam was coming out of my ears." But while Dave might not have been signing Tenacious D on the spot, they were about to take a small but crucial step forward.

Chapter 5

THE BREAKS: TENACIOUS D AND HIGH FIDELITY

Jack starred in two more films before the close of 1997, the first being Richard Sears' stoner flick *Bongwater*. Luke Wilson (brother of Owen) appears as David, a painter and pot seller with no real ambition or motivation. However, when he falls for the spry Serena (Alicia Witt), his life is turned upside down and he ends up pursuing her to New York. Black appears as an acid-toting marijuana farmer, heavily bearded and dishevelled, who meets David on a camping trip. He even manages to squeeze in a performance of 'Jesus Ranch', a song that would later appear on Tenacious D's HBO series. Kyle Gass can also be seen contentedly nodding his head along to Black's lyrical strains. It's only a brief scene, but it serves as an early example of the importance of Tenacious D in Black's career; before their album or even before a record contract, the reputation of the band was helping Black obtain roles. It was to pay off in magnificent fashion just a few years later.

On November 14 of the same year, *The Jackal* was released, directed by Michael Caton-Jones. It features Bruce Willis as a cold and callous assassin, hired to carry out a hit on an anonymous target for the princely sum of $70 million. The FBI, fearing the target may be their director, turn to an Irish sniper (played by Richard Gere), who they believe can identify the assassin. Black stars as Ian Lamont, a technician hired by Willis to build an automated gun mount. He is once again cast as an over-excitable, scruffy and somewhat geeky type. Upon building the mount he attempts to manipulate Willis for more money, and subsequently gets his arm spectacularly blown off. While *The Jackal* didn't work out well for Ian Lamont (Jack's character got killed), it did work out well for Black, given that he had a sizeable role in a film that did exceptionally well, ultimately grossing almost $160 million.

But it was not his film appearances that mark out 1997 as a crucial year in Jack Black's chronology. Since his striking appearances on *Mr. Show*, Jack and Kyle had been in discussion with the show's creators – David Cross and Bob Odendirk – about a possible Tenacious D series. By November 1997 the idea had come to full fruition, with the four writing six fifteen-minute skits alongside other *Mr. Show* contributors, Tom Gianas and Bill Odendirk. HBO put up the cash, and Black and Gass took on the role as executive producers alongside with Cross and Odendirk. Two episodes would be aired back to back, immediately after *Mr. Show*, and first broadcast on November 28. It was entitled, simply, *Tenacious D*.

What is so notable about the series is the huge leap it represents in Black's development, rather than exposure. Prior to this he had been a jobbing actor, moderately successful and building a reasonable head of steam, but his performances in films such as *The Cable Guy* and *Mars Attacks!* display only glimpses of his hyperbolic personality. He notes that this is "by design" as he told Clint Morris of *Moviehole*: "I was always bulging my eyes out, squeezing as hard as I can, and breathing for attention," he remembers. "It's not like natural charisma there, there's a little sweating and bleeding for attention." *Mr. Show* was a chance for Black to display the vibrancy and absurdity of his comic persona, but it was someone else's gig, and he was merely a guest. Now, for the first time, he could allow his *natural* charisma to come through, in a project that he and his best friend had built from the ground up and had utter conviction in.

The series focuses on the band and features many scenarios and exchanges that fans of Tenacious D will be familiar with. Shot in Silvercup Studios, Los Angeles, with just a single camera and tiny budget, it is as raucous, farcical and foul-mouthed as you might expect. The first episode concerns the quest that any credible artist must embark upon – entitled 'The Search For Inspirado'. We see the band desperately trying to write new material but failing entirely, while the time remaining until their next gig is ominously counted down. Come the day of the show, no new material has been produced, and we see JB utterly lose his temper with Kyle. In an explosion of frustration that has become so recognisably Jack Black, he begins shouting and waving his arms emphatically, screaming expletives at Gass, who promptly quits the band. JB can only sob uncontrollably, until the trauma allows him to write a new song. Tenacious D perform it at their regular open mike night and, as becomes a motif of the series, Jack triumphantly knocks down his mike stand when the applause comes in. Episode 2 is entitled 'Angel in Disguise', and the band are once again at one another's throats, but this time over a woman. When Jack sees Kyle cavorting with the object of his affection, a fight breaks out on the street, until a robber threatens her with a gun. A shot is fired, and Kyle dives in front of Jack. Fortunately, Jack had previously given Kyle a 'Friends 4 Ever' Medallion, which takes the bullet. 'Angel in Disguise' also features two notable cameos. The first is David Cross, who staggers into the backstage area before the D go on, dressed as a nun, and cryptically proclaiming, "Well, I killed. Did you see me?" The second is Laura Kightlinger, an American comic who had made her name in the clubs of Boston as a straight-talking, no-nonsense, deadpan comedienne.

She soon turned her talents to writing, however, and as well as various appearances on famed sketch show *Saturday Night Live* (for which she also regularly wrote). Cross and Odendirk had also appeared various times on the program, as had Tim Robbins and Tenacious D themselves; perhaps it was here that Jack and Kightlinger first met. Regardless, they had started dating, and it was a relationship that would last some eight years. She appears as a so-called 'Backstage Betty', approaching the D after another performance at the open mike night. Jack and Kightlinger would appear onscreen together only a few times after this scene, and Black would prove decidedly reticent to reveal details of his private life and relationship with Kightlinger. But despite the contrasting appearance of the couple – the portly Black stands half an inch shorter than the leggy, razor-cheeked Kightlinger – they would become a staple of the red carpets of Black's movies, attempting to outdo one another with their mischievous antics.

Episode 3 is entitled 'Death of the Dream', and it sees the band lose faith in their music when an ex-musician tells them that the rock 'n' roll fantasy is a lie. He compares it to the existence of Sasquatch, but as the boys are in the woods performing mercy killings on their guitars and weeping, they see Bigfoot himself roaming the woods. Reinvigorated by the mysteries of the universe, they take to the stage once more. Sasquatch is played by a heavily made-up John C. Reilly, an American actor who would become a part time player in the so-called 'Frat Pack': starring alongside Black in *Walk Hard: The Dewey Cox Story* (and reprising his role seven years later for *Tenacious D in The Pick of Destiny*). But the highlight of the episode comes when the ex-musician informs the viewer that there are five stages to confronting death: anger, denial, door-to-door rocking, temp job, and acceptance. During 'door-to-door rocking', we see the D knocking on the door of a young mother and performing 'Kielbasa Sausage', championing the joys of sex in a decidedly vulgar manner. Screened alongside 'Death of a Dream' was 'The Greatest Song In The World', the first recording of Tenacious D's most recognisable song, 'Tribute' (though here it is called 'Tribute (To The Greatest Song In The World)'). When a new neighbour rings the police and lodges a complaint about the noise coming from next door, the pair spin the officer a magnificently resourceful – and tuneful – yarn. They claim that whilst on the road they were confronted by a demon, who demanded that unless they played the best song in the world, he would eat their souls. Unabashed, they set about astonishing the demon by performing the best song in the world. However, it is later explained that the song they are singing is in fact only a *tribute* to the greatest song in the world, as they were unable to remember the original. This is the same first song that Tenacious D wrote, inspired by Metallica's 'One', a full three years after its initial conception and debut performance. It operates as a brilliantly fantastical yet concise tale of inter-worldly conflict, all played out within a tight and accomplished musical framework. It is heavily influenced by 'The Devil Went Down to Georgia', a song released by the Charlie Daniels Band on their 1979 album *Million Mile Reflections*. Here, the devil challenges a local fiddle player to a contest of skill, but unable to match the virtuosity of the mortal, he is forced to relinquish his golden violin and return to hell. While Charlie Daniels undoubtedly had his tongue firmly in his cheek when he wrote the song, Tenacious D rework the basic premise for all its comedic potential, modulating from a narrative-led folk verse to a grandiose rock climax with ease. Interestingly, the recording of the song in the episode differs from the recording that would later become so hugely successful for the band – during the middle-eight, Kyle begins to play the opening riff to Led Zeppelin's *Stairway to Heaven*, suggesting that this is in fact the song that defeated the demon, and not Metallica's 'One' or an entirely new composition. However, this variation does not appear in the recording from Tenacious D's debut album. The pair end the tale by explaining that the neighbour in question was in fact the demon, and satisfied with the story (or perhaps simply bemused by its ludicrousness), the officer leaves and the D are free to play another day.

The fifth episode in the series, 'The Fan', is a cunning twist on the conventional stalker concept. The band are approached by a fan named Lee, who seems a little too enthusiastic about the band, even for the hyper-inflated ego of JB. However, upon viewing the fan website he has created, the duo become obsessed with retaining Lee as their number one supporter. To his horror, they break into his house, and Black breathlessly delivers the best line of the episode; "We checked all the hospitals, you weren't in any of 'em." They proceed to perform a song they have written for him, 'Lee', and all three perform 'Special Thing' at the open mike night to close the episode. The actor who plays Lee, Jason Reed, would later tour extensively with the band, playing various roles onstage (including Lee). During the later tour to support Tenacious D's debut album, he would often walk out the front of the venue as fans were queuing. He would be greeted with cacophonous cries of "Lee!", mimicking the duo's pained cries in this episode, a sure signal of the devotion that this short running series inspired.

The final episode of the series is 'Road Gig', and sees Tenacious D invited to play at a club just down the road. However, the band sees this as a momentous milestone, and they take to the road jubilant and confident. When their car runs out of wiper fluid, JB refuses to continue on, and they seek refuge in 'Jesus Ranch' – the compound of a Christian cult. The philosophy of the fanatics is that faeces should be buried rather than flushed away, as it is a part of the soul. At one point, the cult leader explains that the fertile ground produces exceptionally large vegetables, just one of the advantages of living in their own shit. To this, Kyle brilliantly retorts, "What are the others?" The episode also features the first appearance of the 'History Of Tenacious D', which would later appear on the duo's second album as 'History'.

The series was not without its problems. The first two episodes were aired in November 1997, but it was not until 2000 – with the release of *High Fidelity* impending – that the other episodes would finally be shown. Further to this, Gass and Black were offered a full ten-episode run of the series by HBO, but on the condition that they relinquish their position as executive producers. Black recalls on *www.moviehole.com* that this condition as unappealing to the creative instincts of the pair. "They said, 'Yeah, we want to do a lot with you, without you having any creative control. We want you to be more like the Monkees.' We're like, 'What? Why would we want to do that when the first ones were so good with us fuckin' in charge?'" As Kyle remembers that his response was simple; "Fuck you. We'll go make a movie." Jack would later comment that he was pleased they did not make another series, as he was concerned that the pair would "blow their wad" too early. Straightening out the priorities of the band, the two instead opted to focus on getting an album produced.

The TV series, *Tenacious D*, was sadly to go no further, even though it was copiously creative and displayed many, if not all, of the aspects that have made both Tenacious D and Jack Black so successful. It shows a remarkable level of accomplishment; in such short episodes, the character development is clear and effective. Black immediately shines as the boisterous, overly-confident rock star in his own mind; at the end of each performance, he triumphantly knocks over his mike stand in a spontaneous outburst of rock 'n' roll satisfaction. Gass too is immediately recognisable as the more retiring, affable counterpart, who nonetheless displays a degree of focus that takes him beyond mere 'straight guy' status. The relationship between the pair, oscillating from childish camaraderie and mutual respect to unbridled antagonism, is one that has endured throughout Tenacious D's career.

★ ★ ★

Jack's first performance of 1998 wasn't quite as memorable as his last of 1997 – he appeared in the unfortunately titled *Johnny Skidmarks*, though it was mercifully re-named *The Killer Inside* for UK release. A restrained and blackly comic thriller, it is the story of a crime-scene photographer whose lucrative side-line in blackmail embroils him in murder. Jack appeared as Jerry, appropriately portly as a fast-food employee who also becomes involved in the unpleasantness. The cast was strong – Frances McDormand and John Lithgow also appear – but it failed to inspire anything beyond mild interest.

However, Jack did manage to star in two major blockbusters before the year was out, continuing the trend of securing small parts in big movies. The first was the follow-up to 1997's *I Know What You Did Last Summer*, imaginatively titled *I Still Know What You Did Last Summer*. A slasher film content to sit within every boundary the genre suggests, Jack is surrounded by a bevy of willowy girls and muscular boys who are dispatched one by one at the hands of a murderous fisherman. Black was again called upon to play a glassy-eyed, idle type, this time by the name of Titus Telesco (he was un-credited, although it is not clear if this was a deliberate ploy to avoid revealing his cameo before the film was launched). It's fun to see him killed in a suitably gruesome fashion, but in the wake of the smartly self-referential *Scream*, the film relies too heavily on slasher convention to be anything but superficially entertaining. Even the death of the two principal characters at the end couldn't hold back a third instalment, *I'll Always Know What You Did Last Summer*. But much of the film was shot in Culver City, so at least Jack could still visit his mother. Fortunately, his next role was in a far more accomplished film: Tony Scott's *Enemy of the State*. Clearly, Scott had different things in mind for Black since cutting him from *True Romance*, most probably due to his performance in *The Fan* and in Caton-Jones' *The Jackal*. An accomplished and confident spy-thriller, Will Smith stars as a lawyer who becomes an unwitting target of rogue government agents, after he comes into possession of some very sensitive material. It was not to be the last time Black would star with Smith, but at this time he had to be content with a small role as a computer technician in league with the rogue agents. The film was a massive hit, grossing over $250 million.

It was in 1999 that Jack was offered an opportunity that so easily might have changed the course of his career. Jack's performance in the TV series *Tenacious D* hadn't exactly made him a household name, but it had caught the attention of a lot of noteworthy people. One such person was Ben Stiller who, having previous experience of directing Black when he headed *The Cable Guy*, cast Jack in the pilot of a new TV show that Fox were backing. It had been written by Dan Harmon and Rob Schrab, who would later go on to found Channel 101, a high-concept short film project that Black would make various appearances in. But for now, the focus was on *Heat Vision And Jack*. It's an affectionate parody of the types of shows that Jack grew up with; most notably, *The Six Million Dollar Man*, but also *Doctor Who* and *Buck Rogers in the 25th Century*. Black plays Jack Austin (borrowing his surname from the Six Million Dollar Man, Steve Austin), an astronaut who is exposed to dangerous levels of radiation whilst on a mission. Upon returning to Earth he discovers that he has been endowed with superhuman intelligence, but only when the sun is shining. Unfortunately for him, this is a gift that NASA wish to use to their own evil ends. He is forced to go on the run, pursued by a malevolent Ron Silver, who bizarrely plays himself. Accompanying Austin is Heat Vision, Jack's former roommate who merged with his motorcycle when shot by an experimental weapon; voiced by Owen Wilson, he is a loyal companion of Jack's, but unfortunately completely helpless when pushed over.

The pilot opens with Stiller introducing his new show, giving a snide and self-congratulatory spiel about *Heat Vision And Jack*'s brilliance. He remarks to the audience, "As a person you admire, I'm giving you permission to appreciate this show… It's going to knock you back on your coal-mining asses." This pretty much defines the tone of the show; it's silly and bizarre, yet it clearly loves what it mocks, and is just about a close enough likeness to appeal to fans of the originals as well as younger viewers. Black reigns in his usual exaggerated physical comedy to become a (fairly) credible renegade astronaut, his hair neatly quaffed, a leather jacket over his NASA boiler suit. But the show excels most when it slips into almost straight mimicry of 1970s sci-fi series, and then quickly shatters the illusion with a farcical quip or scenario. Early in the episode, its antagonist – a body-snatching alien signal named Paragon – declares to a diner waitress: "Call me master, you worthless monkey whore! All monkey sluts shall be absorbed!" The episode ends with a spectacularly ramshackle shoot-out in a strip club, with Ben Stiller making a cameo as the pirate-styled DJ, and Austin riding off into the sunset in search of more adventure. *Heat Vision And Jack* reunited three actors from the set of *The Cable Guy*: Stiller, Owen and Black. Stiller's reputation had been growing steadily since his MTV series, and in 1998 he had put his directorial ambitions on ice and delivered a breakthrough performance in *There's Something About Mary.* Wilson had also enjoyed some recognition at this point, largely thanks to his performance in Wes Anderson's *Bottle Rocket*, a film which failed commercially but attracted a lot of critical attention. The term Frat Pack was yet to come into common usage, the actors profile's not yet being high enough, the points of divergence not yet regular; but it serves as a testament to the common interests, style and humour of a select group that would later reinvigorate mainstream American comedy.

Despite the pilot of *Heat Vision And Jack* having since gained a significant cult status, Fox decided not to develop the show into a full series, and Black unfortunately missed out on a gig that might have taken him very far indeed. However, watching the pilot, perhaps it was a blessing in disguise. The show works well over its 22 minute running time, but over a series the parody would perhaps become tiresome, the concept possibly too limited to sustain a long-running franchise. Indeed, were Black to have become a TV star at this point, he might have missed out on a better role in a bigger production the year after – a role that would win him as many plaudits as it would roles, and effectively launch his career as a major Hollywood player. With that said, this might not be the last we see of *Heat Vision And Jack* – co-writer Rob Schrab has spoken of a possible feature length, a format the concept would be most suited to. In 2007, on www.wizarduniverse.com, he mentioned a script, saying: "We're still in the draft stage. It's like right now everyone is on board, and Jack wants to do it, and Stiller has his own personal project, but he's saying he loves it and he wants to do it. I just have to get the right script and make sure everyone who wants to be involved with it has the time to do."

1999 held three more film appearances for Jack. The first was *The Love Letter,* directed by Peter Chan, where he had a minor role as a fisherman. Next came the indie flick *Jesus' Son*, directed by Alison Maclean, and starring Billy Crudup as a drug-addled misfit who tells the tale of his trips around America and the eccentrics he has met. One such eccentric is Georgie, a hospital orderly played by Black, who makes his job a little more worthwhile by helping himself to the narcotics on offer in his place of work. The film was a sleeper hit, named by many (including influential critic Roger Ebert) as one of the best films of 1999. The third film was another Tim Robbins production entitled *Cradle Will Rock*, it stars Hank Azaria as a playwright struggling to get his musical staged in the tumultuous climate of depression-era America. Black starred alongside Gass as apprentice ventriloquists, forced into the tutelage of a reluctant Bill Murray. Unlike his restrained approach to the death penalty in *Dead Man Walking*, Robbins took a firm and political position in *Cradle Will Rock,* and it received a mixed critical response. It did not fare at all well at the box office.

It does, however, hold significance for Jack Black. John and Joan Cusack both starred in the film, and with Robbins at the helm and Black in a smaller role, it featured four of the key actors in Jack's next production ... his major breakthrough role: with filming beginning in late 1999, principally in and around Chicago, Black was finally cast in a movie that would catapult him from fringe contender to valuable commodity, Stephen Frears' *High Fidelity*.

Released on March 28, and based on Nick Hornby's 1995 novel of the same name, John Cusack stars as Rob, a record storeowner who has become utterly despondent with the state of his love life. Convinced that every relationship he enters is destined to follow the tragic pattern of his first heartbreak at fourteen, he sets about dissecting his previous relationships. Why is not completely clear; perhaps he hopes to resuscitate his current love affair with Laura, but in his deeply personal and disarming addresses to the camera, he seems more motivated by morbid curiosity and a perverse tendency toward self-emasculation. With his compulsive list-making – in reference to film, music, and relationships – he displays an overwhelming desire to control, and yet he repeatedly allows his neuroticism to overwhelm his rationality, driving away those that he loves. Over the course of the film, we see Rob's relationship with Laura break down, and as he approaches his previous girlfriends to enlighten him as to his failings, it slowly dawns that in his senseless search for new experiences he is paradoxically doomed to repeat himself. The script was immediately appealing to Black: "What I liked about the script," he told *Movie Crazed*, "was its fresh take on relationships. It explores some areas heretofore uncharted in the genre of romantic comedies." Black appears in a role that seems so appropriate it is almost supernatural: Barry is one of Rob's employees, a clerk so élitist in his personal taste and treatment of customers that he verges on fascism. Freewheeling around the store, he gleefully berates the clientele for their inferior knowledge and preferences, refusing sales one minute and forcing them the next. He later joked on EW.com about the difficulty he had in becoming Barry, saying: "It was a tough stretch, sure. I had to wake up every day and look in the mirror and say, 'Hey Barry, how ya doin'? Let's go get some chow. Do you like the same kind of food I do? Because I could go for a QP with cheese.' And Barry would look back and say, 'No, dude, I'm into Big Macs.'" Disparities in diet aside, he delivers the kind of performance that truly makes an actor – the kind of performance that lights up the screen, and the movie builds in electricity and vitality when he appears and notably sags when he leaves. Rob wonders aloud why he keeps his troublesome employee on, but he knows as well as the audience know –

despite his belligerence and zeal, despite his insensitivity and self-involvement, despite even his reluctance to work, he is the kind of character you want around. He is magnetic and dynamic, drawing the attention from all around him, utterly engaging in his manner and verve for life. It's not a profoundly deep performance, but it is a fantastically comic one, allowing Jack for the first time to fully enlist his vivacity within the framework of a well scripted and delivered film. Black's co-star John Cusack perceptively recognised the importance of the performance. "It might be the first time that his talent and a great role have come together with the right director," he told *The Los Angeles Times* in 2000. "It's rare to see someone get as broad and as explosively bizarre as you could possibly want and also break it down and do discreet naturalism with the best of them. That kind of range is dramatic and great." Indeed, it was director Stephen Frears who had insisted on having Black cast as Barry. Black would twice back out of the production, unsure of whether he had the capability the play the role, and twice Frears would convince him to rejoin the fold. "Jack's a bolter," he remarked in *The Guardian*. He also remembers that employees from the studio would make special trips to the cutting room to see the rushes (the unedited, raw footage from a shoot) of Black's scenes, such was the buzz about his performance. It's a rendering that achieves full realisation come the close of the film, when Rob hosts a record launch party and Barry insists he be allowed to play with his new band, Sonic Death Monkey. The film performs the kind of sleight of hand that Tenacious D had been utilising for years – Barry brims with egotism and yet we expect him to be utterly devoid of talent. However, our expectations are defied when he takes to the stage with utter conviction and potency, not to mention a brilliant voice. His band, now dubbed Barry Jive And The Uptown Five, perform a stunning rendition of Marvin Gaye's 'Let's Get It On' that astonishes the crowd at the party and the audience in the theatre alike. Roger Ebert noted that "it is a measure of his acting ability that when he does finally sing in this movie, we are surprised that he can." In fact, the performance was so credible that it drew claims that Black was not actually singing. "It's all me, buddy!" Jack insists. "There's no Milli Vanilli going on here ... No one's ever going to think I sang it, which is frustrating, because I threw down, dude."

While Jack does steal more than his fair share of scenes in *High Fidelity*, the whole film is entertaining and funny, and has the bravura to successfully venture into deeper waters. Cusack's depiction of Rob compellingly combines compassion with selfishness to create the credible portrait of a man peppered with insecurities (although the straight-to-camera addresses, seemingly borrowed from Woody Allen's 1977 classic *Annie Hall*, begin to feel a little artless). It laughs at the irrational level of neuroticism that relationships invariably inspire, and yet never belittles or shies away from the genuine pain of heartache. It's the most involving aspect of the film, and one which Black rightly acknowledges: "Usually, those movies are soft, sentimental and boring. *High Fidelity* has truth and spice."

The movie did well at the box office, grossing over $7 million more than its estimated $20 million budget. Critical response was also favourable, though more than a few reviewers noted that Black was really the film's highlight. Desson Howe of *The Washington Post* remarked, "Whenever he's in the scene, he shoplifts this movie from Cusack." It was also the first time that Jack would be noticed by a few awards bodies – he was nominated for an American Comedy Award, an OFCS (Online Film Critics Society) Award, and a CFCA (Chicago Film Critics Association) Award, all for 'Best Supporting Actor'. He was also nominated for two MTV Movie Awards, one for 'Best Music Moment' – his performance of 'Let's Get It On' – and one for 'Breakthrough Male Performance'. He would ultimately win a Blockbuster Entertainment Award for 'Favourite Supporting Actor in a Comedy or Romance'.

At the movie's launch party in the Sunset Room, California, Tenacious D were asked to play. The huge success of *High Fidelity* and the exposure it particularly brought to Black, was to prove most helpful to the band. The gig at the Sunset Room was overshadowed by a far more important show, however, as the band had set their sights on securing a record deal and cutting an album. In March of the same year, Black and Gass took the Tenacious D show to the famous South by Southwest festival in Austin, Texas, a renowned hotbed of up and coming talent and a hunting ground for music executives and scouts. After a raucous performance at the Austin Music Hall, what can only be described as a bidding war erupted for Tenacious D, with various labels offering escalating advances in the hope of securing Black and Gass' band for their roster. Despite the variety of offers on the table, Kyle claims the choice was obvious: "We took one look at Epic's roster, and we saw Michael Jackson, J. Lo and Celine Dion. We said, 'OK, we've found a home for the D.'" Tenacious D hence signed to Epic and became part of Sony's huge register of artists. Jack has defended their choice to sign to a major label, insisting that the support such a giant corporation could offer the band was far more significant than any money on offer. "It's not for the money 'cos we haven't seen a penny of it!" he jokingly said to Chay Woodman of *www.virtualfestivals.com* in 2003. "But you get the money, and then you get the word spread. You never would've heard of us if it wasn't for the big label signing." However, the pair have also expressed their occasional dissatisfaction with the big label ethos, albeit in a somewhat crude manner. "You have to bend over and get raped by the label," claimed Gass in The Daily Texan. "They never even saw us play, the higher-ups." Regardless, the D had successfully secured a recording contract and could set about taking their hyper-dynamic mock-rock to the masses. Most likely aided by the success of *High Fidelity* and his new record deal, in 2000 Black was also able to purchase a home in Beachwood Canyon in the Hollywood Hills, where he moved with Laura Kightlinger.

It is also reported that at this busy time for Tenacious D, as early as it was in their mainstream career, a film was in the works. British production company Working Title allegedly teamed up with Ben Stiller's Red Hour Films to develop a feature on the D. Two writers from *Mr. Show* – B. J. Porter and Scott Aukerman –

were hired to write the film, with Working Title's Tim Bevan and Eric Fellner and Red Hour's Stiller and Stuart Cornfield down to produce. Reportedly, the premise concerned Tenacious D trying to save the lost city of Atlantis, which was in danger of being crushed by Satan. It was at this crucial time that Tenacious D would fortuitously cross paths with a man named Liam Lynch.

Born in Akron, Ohio as Liam Niederst, he later moved to the tiny city of Hudson, Ohio – the 389th largest city in the American Midwest, to be precise. As is often the case with profoundly creative people, the small town mentality and familiarity became a suffocating influence for Lynch, and he learned to find release in playing the guitar and writing songs. Whilst at school he was enrolled in a program for gifted students, but also diagnosed with a variety of learning difficulties, such as colour-blindness, dyslexia, attention deficit problems and sequential order deficiency. "I'm a watered-down idiot savant," he would later joke to Gil Kaufman of VH1. A high-school guidance counsellor recommended, based on a series of tests, that he become a Circus Manager of a Psychic Advisor. Instead, he spent his teenage years writing his own material and recording it in whatever way he could; given this background, his latterday stellar success is a remarkable personal achievement.

At the age of eighteen he enrolled at Kent State University, where he spent a lot of his time and energy advocating the talents of students with learning difficulties, and conversing with tutors and lecturers about the way in which a student's talent was assessed. But it was in 1996, when Sir Paul McCartney of The Beatles decided to open a performing arts school, that Lynch really came into his own. The new centre, dubbed the Liverpool Institute of Performing Arts, or LIPA, would pick just forty students from around the world to enrol on the first course, and Lynch decided to apply. He had been releasing his own albums since he was 13, so after passing his interview, he simply played some of his songs and demonstrated his talents; he was subsequently chosen as a one of the first ever LIPA students. He was even one of just five guitarists to be handpicked for one-on-one lessons with McCartney himself. He recalls that on his first meeting with McCartney, he informed the ex-bassist and singer that he was forming a Beatles tribute band and looking for a drummer. While at the school he would also have the opportunity to meet such luminaries as Beatles producer Sir George Martin – "the fuckin' Gandalf of recording" – and Brian Eno.

It was while at LIPA that Lynch made his first cautious foray into the world of TV. Looking to accompany some of his and his friend's songs with footage as a Christmas present, he put socks on his hands and filmed the characters miming. The characters were dubbed Sifl and Olly, and from this inauspicious beginning, MTV would ultimately commission two series of *The Sifl And Olly Show*. It would go on to garner a considerable cult following and highlight Lynch as one of the most sought after alternative comedic talents.

Lynch's first part in Jack Black's tale concerns the embryonic Tenacious D movie. The initial concept was never to see the light of day; whilst working at MTV, Lynch would befriend the D and hear concerns about the script they had been offered. He said if they wanted a collaborator, he would be happy to get involved. And so, the genesis of *Tenacious D in The Pick of Destiny* was secured.

However, just as Tenacious D was taking off, Jack Black was about to become a global movie star …

Chapter 6

A LITTLE TURD AND A DEBUT ALBUM

It's difficult not to chronicle the early years of Jack Black's career without the words reading like an extended filmography – this is simply because during these formative years his output was both prolific and varied. The first film he undertook after *High Fidelity* was *Saving Silverman*, a comedy directed by Dennis Dugan and starring Jason Biggs in the eponymous role. While Black's fee for *High Fidelity* remains undisclosed, *Saving Silverman* saw him well and truly inducted into the big leagues with regard to salary. He received $1 million for agreeing to star in the film, although he wasn't entirely happy about this fact being publicised. He didn't want anyone to know that he was receiving such a large sum, saying: "As soon as that was printed, I felt like, 'OK, someone's already started the plot to kidnap me, kill me, and take all my millions.' But whatever, I liked the script." It sees Biggs playing Darren, who is seduced by the domineering and absurdly controlling Judith. She insists he shave her legs, destroy all of his Neil Diamond CDs, and get ass implants; his protests only put his "masturbation privileges" in jeopardy, and he capitulates. However, when she also demands that he can no longer see his friends JD (Black) and Wayne (Steve Zahn), the pair hatch a hackneyed scheme to drive her away from Darren. This scheme involves kidnap, incarceration and the faking of Judith's death, so calamity is most certainly on the cards. The film was not received at all well by critics, who saw its farcical set-ups and boisterous humour as a little off-colour. Peter Bradshaw of *The Guardian*, despite acknowledging Black as a "talented comic," claimed in his review that the film was an "unfunny frat-house mess … which comes very close to … levels of laugh-free awfulness and casual misogyny." However, this seems to be an unfair assessment of the film. Despite having been derided by almost everyone who's seen it – Black himself called the film "a little turd" – the gags are just about frequent and ridiculous enough to keep the film buoyant in its inanity. To accuse the film of near-misogyny almost seems a little squeamish, in fact; it is certainly near to the knuckle, but *Saving Silverman* was in many respects an early prototype to the glut of male-focused comedies that emerged in the 2000s, all of which deal in far worse discourse about the fairer sex but attempt to exonerate themselves with a tacked-on revelation at the end. Jack, however, maintains that he is unhappy with the film, claiming that he only took the role because of his eagerness to keep the ball rolling after *High Fidelity*. "I just got impatient," he says. "I didn't want to wait around for someone else to give me a great part."

Released on February 7, 2001 (Jack's first film of the year), it had the misfortune to be launched on the same weekend as *Hannibal*, the sequel to *The Silence of the Lambs*. This only gave the critics more fuel, Stephen Hunter of the *Washington Post* writing "One thing the makers of *Saving Silverman* do not have to worry about: Hannibal Lecter will never visit them to eat their brains. That is because they have no brains." Either way, the film managed to gross a healthy $26 million. It was released as *Evil Woman* outside of North America.

Black remained hot property in Hollywood despite *Saving Silverman*'s atrocious reception, and yet he next displayed his long running devotion to those that have supported him in the early stages of his career. First he found the time to appear as himself in *The Andy Dick Show*, in the episode 'Flipped'; Andy Dick had been a regular on *The Ben Stiller Show*, and had also appeared in *The Cable Guy* and *Bongwater*. Next, he made a cameo in *Frank's Book,* a short film starring John C. Reilly (who had appeared as Sasquatch in *Tenacious D*) as an office worker who escapes the mediocrity of his existence by dreaming about his notebook. It was directed by R. A. White, The Actors' Gang member who had first recognised Black's talent and insisted he should be cast in *The Big Show.*

Taking a brief break from larger roles, Black was able to concentrate his efforts on Tenacious D's first aural assault on the mainstream public: their debut album. Most of the songs existed in a basic form from the HBO series, and initially it seemed a simple case of committing them to tape. Some new material was written, however, in the manner which Tenacious D had perfected since they first met. "Kyle is always a bubbling cauldron of tunes," Jack said on www.about.com. "He's always playing and working on little melodies and riffs. Then I would need to have something that I think is funny, a concept that I want to riff on, or I need a type of song that I want to make that we've never made before. Then we just start jammin' and we're always recording." However, issues soon emerged. In addition to the success of the series, the cult fanbase that the band had garnered from their famous live shows meant that bootlegs were widely distributed. The band were hence faced with the dilemma of getting their songs to a wider audience without repeating themselves, and offering something new for die-hard fans to engage with.

The first major breakthrough came when LA-based producers the Dust Brothers signed on to record the album. Composed of Michael Simpson and John King, known as 'E.Z. Mike' and 'King Gizmo' respectively, they had first earned renown as hip-hop producers and DJs. In 1996, however, they enjoyed major success with Beck's sophomore effort *Odelay*, and since that time had cemented their position as amongst the most successful producers in the industry. It was Simpson who first expressed an interest in working with the band, although he wasn't absolutely sure that it was a commercially viable option. "I had been a fan of the D for many years," he told Gaby Alter of www.mixonline.com. "I was doing A&R at Dreamworks, and I thought it would be a great idea to do a record with those guys. I wasn't so sure about how well a comedy record would do, but I just felt that based on the shows I'd been seeing, these guys were amazing songwriters, singers and performers, and I thought they could probably make a serious rock record." Their involvement was to have a huge influence on the development of the album. Simpson remembers speaking to the band, and recommending that they form a "supergroup" of sorts: they certainly had enough fans within the music industry to be able to get a credible and talented band together. It was the solution the band had been searching for. No one had heard them play with full backing before – they had only ever performed as an acoustic duo – and the addition of a full band would not only add a new dimension to their sound, but also boost their rock credentials.

The first step was securing a venue for the sessions, and the band first settled on Arch Angel Studios in Los Angeles. The studio was owned by Neil Diamond, who had appeared in *Saving Silverman* as himself; he had even given Black a guitar, with the note, "You're gonna need a good guitar, see you at the top of the charts" written on it. Some initial tracks were laid down here, and Black remembers the studio fondly. "It's like a 1970s living room," he says. "Lots of brown shag carpets, lots of big posters of Neil. It was groovy; had a good vibe to it." But the band soon had to turn their attention to assembling their supergroup. The choice of drummer was obvious, at least in an ideal world. Since their initial meeting with Dave Grohl, Tenacious D had gone on to support Foo Fighters in concert – Dave recalls how "they played 'Fuck Her Gently' and had six or seven thousand people go berserk pre-album. That was under the radar, Cinderella shit!"

Ever more impressed with the band's talents, he had asked them personally to perform a cameo in the Foo Fighter's video for their 1999 single 'Learn to Fly'. The band starred as crooked airplane cleaners who, presumably attempting to smuggle drugs, hide a suspicious looking packet in the coffee machine. All on board the plane except for the Foos become completely incapacitated, and the band are forced to land the plane themselves. It was an appearance that Jack claims "opened the door" – "Then we were able to say, 'Could you do us a little favour?'" Despite their initial scepticism, Grohl did indeed agree to play drums on the record, working with the band for one and a half days. He was also playing with Steven Macdonald, who had played bass in the 1980s and 1990s with Californian rockers Red Kross. The Dust Brothers had Tenacious D run through their entire live set, with Macdonald playing bass, and Grohl improvising drum tracks. King recalls how in the equivalent of a single day of studio time, Grohl managed to lay down twenty songs, all without the aid of a click track to keep time.

Others soon followed suit. Keyboard player Page McConnell, member of jam-rock pioneers Phish signed up, alongside Vandals guitarist and composer Warren Fitzgerald. With the drum tracks successfully recorded, the Dust Brothers took the sessions back to their own studio in Silver Lake, nicknamed 'The Boat'. Here the rest of the album was laid down, with reports from the studio being very positive. Black remembers his enthusiasm of working with King and Simpson, calling them "the best guys in the business," and boldly claiming, "they could make Shakira sound good." In turn, King spoke highly of Black's performance: "He's a great vocalist ... he goes through so many vocal styles." In fact, Black dryly claims that the only challenge in the recording the songs was "trying to figure out how to remove the originality and make them all commercial so they can be hits on the radio." The final mix was done by Ken Andrews after which the album was ready to be released. The whole process was so successful that Black claims he intends to write a book about it: "Blueprint For Success, by Tenacious D," he told *The Daily Texan,* "We'll be outlining exactly what you have to do. First and foremost, you get a major label deal. Get Dave Grohl to play drums, superstars on all instruments, Dust Brothers to produce … it's as easy as one, two, D."

Album opener 'Kielbasa' sets out the stall for the debut perfectly. Beginning with a brief spoken word skit, it then launches into a rock-funk exodus that extols the joys of sex, rock 'n' roll and getting stoned in equally excitable terms. Over its three-minute running time it manages to squeeze in some suitably sleazy wah-guitar and even a sitar-embellished breakdown, heralding the beginning of Tenacious D's determination to ransack every cavern that guitar-based music had marked on the map; where other intrepid rockers were content to explore, preserving the integrity, Tenacious D plunder and pillage.

'Tribute' is featured in all its fully realised glory, the full band treatment emphasising the shift between folk tale and fully blown rock opera. 'Wonderboy' brilliantly parodies rock music's love affair with mythology as JB tells the tale of Wonderboy, his arch nemesis Nasty Man (Gass), and a randomly introduced hydra. 'Fuck Her Gently' is the D's stab at a ballad, which insists that rough sex is the not the way to a woman's heart. With this said, it insists on using terms like 'fuck', 'hump' and 'bone' to expound its theory, as strings melodramatically (and somewhat ironically) flourish around the delicately picked guitar part. Other standout tracks include 'Friendship', which reassures fans that Kyle and Jack will remain friends for as long as they have a record deal; 'Double Team', a hilarious invocation of sexual prowess that moves from cloying opening to muscular synth-funk middle-eight to a strident riff-driven conclusion; and album closer 'City Hall', which sees Black and Gass take complete control of the masses before their bickering leads them to poison one another.

What's most surprising about the album is its utter conviction from start to finish. The song writing is confident and assertive, and even with all the pomposity and ridiculousness, it shocks the listener with its approachability. The songs are direct, hook-laden affairs, and if Black and Gass weren't so opposed to the dour sincerity of songwriters, they might have a serious shot at becoming them. Lyrically the album is predictably giddy and inane, but the strength of the tunes is such that it feels more like deliberate parody, and the album is elevated above mere joke status. The sketches that appear intermittently do have a negative bearing on the album's force, however. Familiarly purposeless and salacious, they draw heavily on the patter of the HBO series, but fail to raise more than a smirk without a visual element. On successive listens they simply become an irritation, considerably slowing the pace of the record.

Released on September 25, 2001, the album received mixed reviews from the press. *Rolling Stone* grandly proclaimed that "now is the hour of Tenacious D, standing tall on rock's Mount Olympus with their acoustic guitars and a songbook full of pure stoner poetry," and gave the album three and a half out of five stars. *Time* magazine noted how they "set themselves up as buffoons … then proceed to defy expectations with precise guitars, polished vocal harmonies and slamming backup musicians," as well as praising their "boundless capacity for self-mockery that makes the most professional rockers look like solemn poseurs." *The Independent*'s review, however, was particularly scathing, calling the album "curiously bereft of even the slightest skidmark of humour," it claimed that the "one joke is the yawning gap between the duo's minimal talent and the colossal egotism of their fanciful self-mythologizing", and attributed the very existence of the album to Jack's celebrity slipping out of control. It was not an immediate hit either, peaking at just Number 33 in the US Albums Chart with 42,000 sales, and 38 in the UK Albums Chart. A brief attempt to recall the CD from stores, due to its depiction of two babies chained to a pillar on which Satan is standing, probably didn't help either.

However, the album's first single 'Tribute' would soon change its dwindling fortunes. Released in July of the following year (following the publicity Jack received from *Shallow Hal*), it was accompanied by a superb Liam Lynch directed video, which saw

Dave Grohl playing the part of the devil and almost unrecognisable under heavy makeup. Right from the offset, the atmosphere on set was very positive, with Kyle Gass declaring, "I think it's gonna be fantastic, but I don't wanna jinx it." It is essentially a higher budget remake of the HBO episode that features 'Tribute', except the narrative framing device is the band entering a karaoke booth to record their song. Grohl was first on set in order to undergo hours of make-up for his transformation into a devil – but despite the patience necessary, his performance no doubt did much for the video's exposure. Eagle eyed viewers can also catch a glimpse of director Liam Lynch and Jack's buddy Ben Stiller at the end of the video, when the duo burst out of the booth to the alarm of passing shoppers. Following the huge success of this video – it became the most requested clip on *Kerrang!* TV in 2002 – the album was then certified gold in America and silver in the UK by September 2002. Black was a little put out by the album's success in the UK, remarking, "I'm a little embarrassed about the silver. Is it wrong if we don't accept it? ... I don't want anyone mistaking my silver for platinum. That's why it's imperative we make it to gold." Fortunately, by December it had indeed made gold. The following year the band shot a video for 'Wonderboy' with esteemed filmmaker Spike Jonze, director of such oddities as *Being John Malkovich* and *Adaptation*. The video is an epic fantasy adventure, that sees the band clad in medieval garb in an icy wasteland, battling the elements as well as an unseen creature. Director Jonze remarked that "It just seemed appropriate, the song was epic, the video needed to be epic ... You can't short-change the D." Jack and Kyle even had pal John C. Reilly on set for support. The single reached 24 in the UK singles chart. Following the slow-burning success of the album, the D embarked on a US tour – their second ever – once again they stripped down their act to just the duo and their acoustic guitars, "to hoard in all the money possible". Their set would include covers of Queen's 'Flash Theme' and The Beatles' 'You Never Give Me Your Money', as well as appearances from Sasquatch, Spiderman and Osama Bin

Laden (all played by cohort Jason Reed). Following their own tour, they headed out in support of US bands Jimmy Eat World and Weezer for a thirteen-date stint as openers on the triple bill.

★ ★ ★

After his brief dalliance with smaller roles, and with Tenacious D's debut effort out in the public arena, Black was able to return to the movie mainstream and score his first leading role – in the Farrelly Brother's *Shallow Hal*. The Farrelly Brothers had earned their keep as the kings of so-called 'gross out' comedy; films such as *There's Something About Mary* and *Me, Myself and Irene*, whereby bodily excretions, sexual mishaps and repellent physical conditions are all fair game in the name of laughs. With *Shallow Hal*, however, they edged away from the wince-inducing scenarios that had made them successful and towards a warmer, gentler tale of love and acceptance. It was a major move for Black. Prior to this, he had imagined a career trajectory as a character actor, cropping up in supporting roles, but he had not envisaged appearing in films where he was the main focus and draw. His scene-stealing turn in *High Fidelity* soon changed that, however. He notes that the transition required a change of style, a more deliberate, calculated approach to acting: "When you're coming in for a little character part, there's so much pressure to pack a huge wallop into the one day that you're working or whatever. It would be hard to sustain that kind of insane energy for a whole movie. I don't think I would want to actually, because that would be an annoying performance." Black states that he enjoyed the *Shallow Hal* experience, the atmosphere on set being "like a family barbeque", though he found the added pressure of leading man status quite trying. "The hours are pretty bad," he told www.tenaciousjoes.com. "If you don't like to get up, it's bad. They wake you up at like 5:30 in the morning… And I was in every goddamn scene in the movie."

Black stars as the title character, Hal Larson, a man haunted by the dying words of his father: "Hot young tail – that's what it's all about." Determined to make his daddy proud, Hal becomes a womanizing lothario, refusing to commit to anything beyond meaningless sexual dalliances and yet willing to say anything to experience them. With the aid of his pal Mauricio, played by *Seinfeld*'s Jason Alexander, he frequents the local hotspots in town, mercilessly rejecting all but the most beautiful of women. On one fateful day, however, he is trapped in an elevator with an urban guru of sorts, who tells Hal he will charm him to be more attractive to the opposite sex. However, he in fact hypnotises him to project inner beauty externally – i.e., to see nice people as attractive, regardless of how hideous they may actually be.

Under the impression that he is now irresistible to the opposite sex – of course he is simply trying it on with more approachable women – he bumps into Gwyneth Paltrow's Rosemary and begins wooing her. She is initially sceptical, having never been the object of this level of attention before – mainly because she is somewhat on the large side, weighing in at around twenty stone. She's beautiful inside, however, and so Hal sees her this way outside; the pair embark on a sweet and endearing love affair. Black has hinted that the chemistry on screen was not quite matched by the chemistry off. He says the pair got on fine on set, but "I didn't really see her off the set. She'd go to her trailer and I'd go to mine." From here on, the film shoehorns in various comedic capers based around obesity – chairs breaking, big splashes at the swimming pool, large amounts of food being consumed, and so on. Hal is baffled, of course; at one point, Rosemary throws Hal her underwear, which despite having looked like a skimpy arrangement on her body, now look around six foot in circumference. He doesn't dwell on these complexities, merely telling her, "Come here, Houdini!"

Of course, this joyous arrangement can't continue indefinitely, and Mauricio searches out the guru and insists the charm be lifted. He duly obliges, and when Hal sees Rosemary in her true form, he is sent reeling. Naturally, however, he realises the error of his ways, makes a heartfelt gesture of repentance, and all in the audience are sent home happy. Black's performance is certainly more restrained than many of his previous turns, and it was a role he found difficult at first. "It was hard for me to be a regular character, an everyday Joe," he notes. "Usually I play tweaked psychos ... That's my comfort zone. It was a challenge in this one, just kinda being normal."

It might be argued, however, that Hal is not quite as normal as Black would have it, and the film not as wholesome. Many critics have picked up on the fact that while *Shallow Hal* masquerades as a slightly outlandish but essentially innocent romantic comedy, at its heart it seems to have split loyalties. The Farrelly Brothers attempted to incorporate their more unforgiving, ruthless comedy into a more palatable framework, but in doing so, they deeply compromised both. The romantic element of *Shallow Hal* invariably leaves a bitter taste in one's mouth because inner worth is still figured in a bodily way, and despite Hal's renunciation of his superficiality at the close of the film, the fact remains that he required the initial incentive of physical attraction to understand Rosemary's inner beauty. Similarly, the more edgy elements of the Farrelly's humour are necessarily watered down, so as not to seem incongruous or discordant with the rest of the film. The film therefore fails to succeed on either level. As Peter Bradshaw noted in *The Guardian*, *Shallow Hal* relies on "an equation that takes a lot of provocative chutzpah to carry off and in any case only makes sense in an uncompromisingly black-comic film – not this sentimental MOR exercise." Ever honest about his projects, Black has since expressed regret about the way *Shallow Hal* turned out. "I feel I kind of sold out a little bit," he stated in *Playboy*. "I had an opportunity to work with some dudes I thought were really funny, but it didn't turn out as I'd hoped. I wasn't proud of it, and I got paid a lot of money, so I guess in retrospect it feels like a sell out." Gwyneth Paltrow has expressed similar feelings about the picture, stating in a Guardian interview that she classed *Shallow Hal* as one of her "shite" films. However, not all were so downcast about the film. Roger Ebert gave a more sympathetic review of the picture, pointing out that it's just not commercially viable to hire Gwyneth Paltrow and have her in a fat suit *all* the time; he also notes that in the world of cinema, things have to be realised in a visual way, and therefore the Farrelly brothers were severely limited in the manner they rendered Rosemary's inner beauty. Box office figures were very good with the film grossing over $70 million, a full $30 million over its estimated $40 million budget. Black also found for the first time that his acting career was being associated closely with his film career, though not with the most favourable results. "It was a bummer after *Shallow Hal* when people were carrying around the *Shallow Hal* billboards at the concerts," he said on www.about.com. "That's not really heavy metal, to look out in the audience when you're trying to rock and there's a *Shallow Hal* cardboard cut-out." Nonetheless, he had the dubious honour of being nominated for a Teen Choice Award for his performance in the film.

Jack must have ended 2001 with mixed emotions. Tenacious D had graduated from underground heroes to mainstream marvels, their album selling hundreds of thousands of copies globally, their tour regularly selling out 2,000 seat venues, and the video for 'Tribute' propelling them to superstar status. Despite the inherent non-conformity of the act, their peculiar brand of mock folk-rock storytelling, littered with in-jokes and pop culture references, crudity and inanity, had found a considerable mainstream audience. Similarly, Jack's acting career had taken a leap he would never have predicted himself. At 5' 7", hairy and rotund, Black had forced his way into the ultra-élite circle of Hollywood leading men; amongst the super-abundance of chiselled jaws and muscular physiques vaguely connected to being an actor, Jack shone as a beacon of talent, personality and downright humour. And yet, he had expressed disappointment about his first leading man role, feeling that the film had not turned out as he wanted it to be. In fact, some felt he had not been in a great film since *High Fidelity*, and the pressure amongst critics was mounting to see if he would ever live up to the promise he had shown in that breakthrough film.

Chapter 7

GRADUATING FROM THE SCHOOL OF ROCK

Jack's first booking of 2002 saw him retuning to the silver screen for *Orange County*. It was written by screenwriter Mike White, who had been Jack's neighbour for three years in LA and his friend ever since. White had grown up in LA's Pasadena suburb, and gone on to attend Wesleyan University in Connecticut with the aspiration of becoming a New York playwright. However, he was offered an opportunity through a connection at college to work in Hollywood, and so he moved back to LA. White had first worked on *Dawson's Creek* as a writer and producer, but gone on to garner critical acclaim as the writer and star of the creepy, blackly comic *Chuck and Buck:* a story about a playwright who becomes obsessed with an old school friend. In *Orange County*, White created a sweet yet intelligent coming-of-age tale about the restrictive presence of home and the need to fly the coop. It was the first major casting for Colin Hanks, son of Tom, who stars as Shaun Brumder, an overachieving, wildly talented teen with aspirations of becoming a novelist. He has written a manuscript that he hopes will be good enough to secure himself a place at Stanford University, where he will be under the tutelage of his literary hero, Marcus Skinner. However, his bumbling guidance counsellor sends the wrong letter under his name, and he is rejected. Desperate to escape the dysfunctions of his family and suffocating influence of his dim-witted friends, he embarks on a journey to convince the tutors at Stanford of their mistake. Black features as Shaun's drug-addled brother Lance, a troublesome stoner who is just about lucid enough to see that he wants to help Shaun, but not quite lucid enough to actually do so. It must have seemed like familiar territory for Black; it was just the kind of role he had played in *Bongwater* or *Jesus' Son*, the kind of "tweaked outsider" character that Jack revels and excels in. He brings a level of depth to the character beyond mere comic superficiality, and amidst the misfits and no-hopers that populate the film, Lance is most illustrative of the imperfect yet sincere companionship that Orange County offers Shaun. He staggers through the film in a semi-articulate reverie, and beyond a few predictable set pieces (like a guest nearly drinking the drug-free piss he has acquired for his parole officer), he provides most of the laughs and a good deal of the heart of the film. His excitable, ungainly style of physical comedy is well in evidence here, but it is when he tones down this mania for a more dialogue-driven scene that his charisma as a comic performer truly shines through. Toward the end of the film, he becomes partly responsible for burning down a part of Stanford University, and is confronted by an inquisitive fireman (played by Ben Stiller). Wide-eyed and feigning bemusement, he desperately attempts to lie his way through the interview before turning tail and running – and what is most enjoyable about the performance is Lance's complete hopelessness interjected with the occasional glimpse of guile.

By now, this natural force of character was something that was being noticed by everyone who Jack worked with, both on and off screen. Star Colin Hanks remarked, "the guy is a genius,"

Jack with co-star Brittany Murphy in the 1997 comedy, *Bongwater*.
Everett/Rex Features

Jack aka Barry in everyone's favourite *High Fidelity* scene, 2000.
W. Disney/Everett/Rex Features

Jack and Kyle arrive at the Tenacious D *Complete Masterworks* DVD premier in typical low-key fashion, New York, November 2003.
Rex Features

Jack as Dewey Finn in 2003's *School of Rock*.
Paramount/Everett/Rex Features

On the set of *King Kong* with director Peter Jackson, 2005.
Universal/Everett/Rex Features

As the Writers Guild of America strike reaches its second week, Jack joins the picket lines outside Universal Studios, November 13, 2007. *Finalpixx/Retna*

Timid as ever, Jack/Po shows off his Kung Fu skills at the premier of *Kung Fu Panda* in Los Angeles, June 1, 2008. *Sipa Press/Rex Features*

Taking time to sign fan autographs at the
Kung Fu Panda DVD launch, Los Angeles, November 9, 2008.
Alex J. Berliner/BEI/Rex Features

Tenacious D perform on *The Tonight Show With Jay Leno* in the same outfits that wowed festival-goers in the summer of 2008.
NBCUPHOTOBANK/Rex Features

Jeff 'Fats' Portnoy with the all-star cast of 2008's *Tropic Thunder*.
Dreamworks/Everett/Rex Features

Jack and wife Tanya Haden at the 17th annual BAFTA/La Britannia awards, proving he can dress to impress, Los Angeles. November 6, 2008.
Alex J. Berliner/BEI/Rex Features

If ever a photograph can summarise an actor's maverick personality ...
Jack Black totally unfazed by the massed ranks of the paparazzi at the 61st Cannes Film Festival, May 15, 2008.
Sipa/Rex Features

saying: "It may not look like he does much, but I think he's one of the funniest individuals on the face of the planet. And I've been a fan of his for so fucking long, I mean for years... Even when he's not trying to be funny, he's hysterical." While *Orange County* is far more than the puerile teen comedy some assumed it would be, it really softens its bite with an overly sentimental ending, thereby missing the opportunity to become the highly esteemed indie film that it had the potential to be. Even with an exclusive Foo Fighters single on the soundtrack, and an accompanying promo featuring clips from the movie, *Orange County* failed to capture the public's attention. It did well at the box office, comfortably clearing its budget, but it remains an agreeable yet ultimately forgettable experience.

Jack's next film was to be his first foray into animation, and it would prove a lucrative aspect of his career in the future. Since the 1990s, computer technology had been playing a larger and larger role in the development of big budget Hollywood films. Movies such as Ridley Scott's *Jurassic Park* displayed the potential of CGI (computer generated imagery) with extended sequences entirely reliant on computer graphics, allowing filmmakers to render something fundamentally unrealistic in a realistic manner.

It was not until 1995 that anyone had the foresight to recognise the true potential of computer animation beyond its function in live action films, and as a form in its own right. It was Disney, who had pioneered and pushed traditional forms of animation into the mainstream in the early twentieth century, who teamed up with California-based Pixar Animation Studios to produce the first entirely CGI animated film: *Toy Story*. The film tapped into an enduring childhood fantasy – that toys have a life of their own that they hide from their human counterparts – to develop a tale of friendship and adventure that enjoyed widespread critical acclaim and monumental box office success alike. The film was vital in the establishment of entirely CGI films in two ways: firstly, it gave CGI a visual identity, allowing it to be stylistically distinct from both conventional animation and live action, yet at the same time it did not attempt to emulate either. Instead, it drew upon the established camera movements and techniques of live action, and the creative capabilities of animation, to create a whole new media with its own features and conventions. Secondly, it set a trend for CGI that must have seemed ambitious at the time, but has since become an established ideal for the form: the film was appealing to both children and adults. It is a warm and tender tale, drawing on tried and tested themes of enemies being forced by circumstance into cooperation. But the humour had a depth that resonated with adults too, with the script sharp and smart enough to have parents happy to take their children back for a second viewing. All of this contributed to the film's runaway success, and it heralded the birth of a new, exceptionally lucrative sector of the industry. Director John Lasseter was even awarded an Academy Special Achievement award in 1996 for "the development and inspired application of techniques that have made possible the first feature-length, computer-animated film."

It was inevitable that after this huge breakthrough, a whole series of computer-animated films would flood the market. The pictures inevitably varied in quality, but the labour intensity and high cost required to produce them generally dictated that the films remained above a certain standard. After *Toy Story*, there was a string a highly successful CGI films, with Pixar offering the likes of *A Bug's Life* and *Toy Story 2*, and Dreamworks producing *Antz* and the brilliant *Shrek*. The genre was also attracting a galaxy of stars, as the nature of production meant that voice recording would be spread out over a long space of time, with a comparatively small amount of sessions necessary to wrap a picture. The huge sums of money being offered since *Toy Story*'s impact no doubt also had an influence. At the turn of the Millennium, voicing a major computer generated film was becoming the hallmark of an established acting career – Mike Myers had voiced Shrek, Tom Hanks had voiced Woody in *Toy Story*, and by the time *Antz* was in production, Woody Allen, Sharon Stone, Gene Hackman, Sylvester Stallone, Jennifer Lopez and Christopher Walken had all signed on to voice a character. It is not surprising, then, that when Black was offered the role of Zeke in *Ice Age*, he accepted.

The film is the tale of a motley herd of pre-historic creatures, forced to band together by the perils of the Ice Age; Manfred, a mammoth, Sid, a sloth like creature, and Scrat, a kind of squirrel. In the midst of the chaos is a human baby, hunted by a vicious pack of sabre-toothed big cats, and protected by the unlikely heroes of the film. Black's character Zeke is one of the tiger-like creatures, as mangy and ugly as he is villainous, who cowardly follows the orders of pack leader Soto without question. At the time of the film's release, Jack was really one of the biggest stars in the credits, though due to the length of production for CGI films, he was far less so when he signed up. He fits perfectly into a more family-orientated film, the spirited and vibrant character of his voice still compelling and entertaining without swearing and vulgarity. It was essentially the first family film that Black appeared in, and the success of his performance must have roused his interest in acting for a younger demographic. In retrospect, Black seems like an obvious choice for these types of roles, but in 2002 this was far from the case. With Tenacious D he was constantly espousing the joys of sex and drug use – a short film made to be shown at gigs even featured him enthusiastically fellating Kyle Gass. His film appearances had not been a huge amount tamer, with many notable for their impressive grasp of English-language profanity and lewdness. It was therefore a bold move for Blue Sky Studios, the creators of *Ice Age*, to cast Jack in a role where he could not use vulgarity to get a laugh. It also proved an intelligent one, however, when he excelled in the part and proved there was far more to his appeal than mere shock tactics. The film was a huge success, grossing just under a colossal $400 million worldwide, though critical response was not as fawning as it was for the likes of *Toy Story* or *Shrek*. In truth, the concept was not as engaging and the script simply not as funny. Black did not reprise his role for the second film.

As if to deliberately pick the exact opposite role to the one he had just completed, Jack's next move was to return to live action cinema and to the company of David Cross and Bob Odendirk. He appeared in what was essentially the *Mr. Show* film, entitled

Run Ronnie Run! It was a feature length adaptation of one of *Mr. Show*'s most popular characters, Ronnie Dobbs, a mulletted miscreant who is constantly being arrested for his petty scams and hi-jinks. Black starred as the lead chimney sweep in a sketch clearly based on Mary Poppins, although we are helpfully told by the narrator that the scene was cut from the final release of the musical it was allegedly shot for. Singing a song colourfully entitled 'Give Her a Kick in the Cunt', Black adopts a suitably exaggerated Cockney accent and advocates booting a lady friend in the groin as the best means of irritating her. As juvenile as this may seem, it in many respects demonstrates Black's versatility; he has an almost bi-polar approach to comedy, which takes in playful tomfoolery, frat-house style bawdiness, subtler script-led pieces and an electric physicality. This wide range of skill and charisma allows him to take on a children's film, such as *Ice Age*, and a distinctly adult sketch such as the aforementioned, and succeed in investing both with his own particular charm. Nonetheless, Black maintains that the eclectic range of roles he chooses are not consciously selected for their variation. "I think when it comes to different audience demographics, I can't control it," he said to www.ign.com, "so I'm just like, 'Ah, whatever.' I just work on cool things." Despite the brilliance of the scene in which Jack Black performs, *Run Ronnie Run!* unfortunately went a similar way. Cross and Odendirk became increasingly isolated from the post-production process, with Cross ultimately disassociating himself with the film. It never saw a theatrical release; it was shelved for two years by New Line Cinema, before being released direct-to-video in 2003. It failed to make much impact, though Jack's song did win a DVD Exclusive Award for 'Best Original Song in a DVD Premiere Movie.'

As a barometer of Jack's rising fame, his next step was to host the MTV Movie Awards in the June of 2002. A younger, more anarchic take on the classic movie awards show template, the MTV Movie Awards had been enjoying an increasing influence over the film industry since its inception in 1992. Movies were being increasingly tailored to, and influenced by, the so-called

'MTV Generation', a demographic principally consisting of teens, more accustomed to the techniques of fast cuts and non-linear narrative methods used in music videos, and fluent in the language of American pop culture. In conjunction with the success of MTV, the teen movie grew in prominence, focusing on the now established coming-of-age concerns of first love, sex, rebellion and angst. And in response, MTV launched its own awards show to tap into the huge market for teen movies – indeed, it was MTV's own production company that had financed *Orange County.* Previous hosts of the show include Will Smith, Mike Myers and Black's friend Ben Stiller; but Jack was down to host alongside Sarah Michelle Gellar, who had risen to fame as star of the vampire-teen TV drama *Buffy The Vampire Slayer.* As is the custom of the Awards, the pair also starred in parodies of that year's biggest films: on this occasion *Spider-Man, Lord of the Rings: The Fellowship of the Ring* and *Panic Room.* The sketches cleverly cut in footage from the original with newly recorded material, to create the illusion that the hosts of the show are interacting with characters from the film. The *Spider-man* sketch was chosen to open the show, and sees Peter Parker (played by Toby McGuire) bitten by a radioactive spider as per the original. However, it is not McGuire but Jack Black who awakes the next morning, and his surprise is evident upon examining his new physique in the mirror: "Oh, my god … I'm totally freaking hot!" His costume goes through various versions, each rejected for being "not gay enough," until he finally settles on the classic Spider-man outfit ("exactly the right amount of gay"). Jack's Spider-man is not quite the figure of morality and heroism that Stan Lee imagined in his Marvel comic, however. He decides he will "get to the community stuff later," instead opting to draw Yoda on his chin and get off with Sarah Michelle Gellar. The skit is, frankly, bizarre.

The *Lord of the Rings Parody* is similarly outlandish, and sees Black meeting with all the guardians of the ring. However, he dutifully informs the ensemble that "last night, me and some buddies had a little too much mead," and that he has had the ring that is the focus of the story attached to his penis via a Prince

Albert piercing. Unable to remove the ring, Sarah Michelle Gellar is forced to rip it out, with the triumphant declaration of "Let's get this bitch to Mount Doom."

After the MTV Movie Awards, Black next returned to the underground to guest on a few friends' projects. He first voiced a character for the MTV show *Clone High*, a cartoon about a high school whereby all of the students are clones of famous historical figures. The show featured various special guests over its one season run, including Jack's friend Andy Dick. Jack voiced Larry Hardcore in Episode 8, entitled 'Raisin' The Stakes: A Rock Opera in Three Acts'. Next, he appeared on Liam Lynch's *Fake Songs* album, singing on the track 'Rock and Roll Whore'. 'Rock 'n' Roll Whore' is a raw, Zeppelin-esque riot, Black delivering the nonsensical lyrics with his distinctive emphatic roar over buzz-saw guitar riffs.

During 2003, Black also teamed up with some old friends to become involved with the newly-developed Channel 101 film festival. Channel 101 is a short film project that mimics the dynamics of the TV industry, whereby participants can send in films, they are played at a monthly showing, and audience members decide which to green light for more episodes and which to cancel. The concept, which largely airs on the internet, had been created by the previously mentioned Dan Harmon and Rob Schrab. Black had previously worked with the pair on *Heat Vision and Jack,* where they were both writers and executive producers of the pilot. Harmon and Schrab also both produced their own short films to enter into the festival, and in 2003 Harmon created *Computerman*. It stars Black in the title role as a half-man, half-computer, created when Harmon's character Eugene cuts his finger and his DNA fuses with his desktop computer. However, in keeping with the lo-fi spirit of Channel 101, costume only goes as far as Black in his underpants, wearing a monitor on his head and strapping a keyboard to his chest. Over six five-minute episodes, the naïve and child-like Computerman and his creator Eugene are pursued by a corrupt FBI agent hell-bent on anally raping Eugene and harnessing Computerman's powers for his own ends. After three episodes, fearing cancellation by a wearied public, the show reinvented itself as a science fiction epic, and when that got old, the main characters were killed off and sent to a poorly animated heaven. By this time *Computerman*'s time was up and it was cancelled at a showing in January 2004.

In June 2003, Black would appear in his second Foo Fighters video, but this time his role was a lot more central and infinitely more risqué. The video was for 'Low', the third single from the Foo's fourth album *One By One* (and only the second video not the feature the band performing the song). It serves as a distinctly adult home-video: as the clip begins, we see Black and Grohl pulling into a decidedly sleazy motel, both sporting trucker caps and tatty clothes. After a brief exchange – "What's up, Lester?", "What's up, Cole?" – the pair disappear into a room and the taut, boisterous opening riff kicks in. The style of the video switches to hand-held, and we witness what appears to be an intimate but regular get-together for the two characters. While it begins with the pair engaging in distinctly masculine activities, manically dancing around and arm wrestling, after the booze starts flowing things take a bizarre turn. Grohl opens a suitcase to reveal a collection of women's clothing, including stilettos, wigs and underwear. The pair don their new outfits, make up and all, and proceed to engage in a variety of alcohol-fuelled, semi-sexual, semi-violent acts. One particularly strange shot sees Black spanking a prone Grohl, in night-vision green, with a strobe light on.

Come the close of the video, we see Black clearly not feeling his best and vomiting in the toilet, before Grohl escorts him to bed and passes out himself. The two remerge the following morning, share a hand slap and a knowing nod, and go their separate ways. The somewhat lurid content of the video saw MTV banning it from their daytime playlist, but in an interview with *Kerrang!* magazine, Dave and Jack seemed little bothered. They spoke of the "you scratch this and I'll scratch that" dynamic of their relationship, with Kyle referring to Jack's performance in the 'Low' video as the "ultimate pay off." "You had a boner that entire video!" he accused, to which Grohl replied, "What are you gonna do? He's hot."

During this time, Black had also starting work on a new film that showed considerable promise. His friend Mike White, of *Orange County* fame, had written it specifically for him. Mike remarks that, as a friend and a fan, "I felt like there was an opportunity to write something for him that would show different colours of him than he's been able to show in some of the other movies he's done." White was particularly interested in the duality of his career, as both an actor and a musician, and even referred to Jack as "the perfect anti-hero for our times." White even compared him to one of Black's most revered heroes, commenting that he had the kind of dynamism and unhinged energy of Gene Wilder in *Charlie and the Chocolate Factory*, and that the idea of Jack jamming with a group of kids kept recurring to him. Nonetheless, he was not blind to the apparent disparity appearing in Black's back catalogue; that while he made his name as an "adult' entertainer, far too rich in topic and tone for young eyes and ears, he was slowly edging into the world of mainstream, family entertainment. He agreed that there was a general perception that Black was "too risqué" for children, but was assured in his faith that people would come around, commenting that it would simply take the power of word of mouth to convince sceptics Black was an able and suitable family entertainer.

White's concept was that Black's passion for rock music could be incorporated seamlessly into a film, even though he admits that he has no interest in classic rock himself. The script that resulted from White's premise concerned a struggling musician, named Dewey Finn, who manages to get a position as a teacher in an exclusive private school. However, he soon rewrites the curriculum to give a comprehensive education in rock. The film was to be called *School of Rock*, and right from its inception everything seemed to be coming together. White had a history of having to battle to get his projects developed, but *School of Rock* was green-lit with an early draft of the script and Jack's participation. Jack had expressed his pleasure in receiving a script that stood out from the throng – one which didn't cast him as some "aging frat guy." He even ventures that writing is both the hardest and most important element of creating a film, and laments that writers are the worst paid and most underappreciated contributors to a picture (this comment now stands as a kind of prophetic foretelling of the Writers Guild of America strike that would bring Hollywood to a halt in 2007-2008). The lead character himself certainly appealed to Black as well: "Dewey is basically me five years ago, when I was desperate, frustrated and had no career," he claimed at the time. Similarly impressed with the screenplay was director Richard Linklater, who was next to sign on, and the film immediately took another leap in promise and potential. Richard Linklater was and remains a respected alternative filmmaker; since his breakthrough movie *Dazed and Confused* in 1993, he had garnered a reputation as one of the freshest talents in American independent cinema, and his movies always rattled along to a great rock 'n' roll soundtrack. Linklater remarks that the script had a personal significance for him: "I am a big fan of Jack and Mike," he says. "And Jack's character, a struggling musician willing to do almost anything to help realise his dreams, reminded me of my formative years as a filmmaker."

With all of the necessary pieces in place, filming began, and Jack couldn't have been more optimistic about the film's prospects. It had been written specifically for him not only by a close friend, but also a talented and acclaimed writer, and he was also a huge fan of Linklater: "This is a cream-dream," he remarked to Kim Morgan at www.reel.com at the time. Jack moved to New York and lived with Mike White for the duration of production, which was an experience White was somewhat bemused by. During one particular bout of madness, the toilet in their apartment exploded while the fire alarm was sounding, prompting Black to run around containing the chaos dressed only in his underwear. "I thought: *I'm living in a Jack Black movie*,"

White remembered on www.citybeat.com. But White also recalls that Black was a consummate professional, always preparing for his day on set and arriving ready to turn in the best performance possible. According to White, the atmosphere on set was light-hearted and jocose, a contrast to the usual stress and tension of a big-budget, tight-schedule production. It served as a reminder for White as to why he first got involved in film; because it is *fun*. For Jack, the film was also very enjoyable, but it proved a challenge the likes of which he had not yet encountered. This was only his second role as a leading man, and it was considerably more demanding that what he'd faced with *Shallow Hal*. After filming he referred to it as both the most fulfilling and most difficult experience of his professional career. The pressure he felt almost seems manifest in his increased level of swearing: "I've never had to work this hard," he told Kim Morgan, "because it wasn't just fuckin' acting in every scene but it was also fuckin' freaking out about the music in every scene … And if the music sucked, especially the stuff I had to sing, it would have been a fuckin' disaster. So there's a lot of extra stress along with the pleasure."

School of Rock has become the film that has defined Jack Black, and his character Dewey Finn is nothing less than an alter-ego: a role that Black himself couldn't have better envisaged and written. When he is unanimously voted out of his own adult band 'No Vacancy' for general buffoonery, ruining every song with excessive soloing and channelling the power of rock in the most exaggerated way imaginable, he takes to his bed to lick his wounds. Unfortunately for him, his roommate Ned (played by Mike White) is continually being harassed by his overbearing girlfriend to kick Dewey out, who is well behind on rent payments and little more than a nuisance. Ned and Dewey previously played in the aptly named Maggot Death Eater together, but Ned had long since abandoned his aspirations of fame and settled into a life of domesticity. He gives Dewey a pep talk, telling him that it is time to put his dreams of superstardom to bed and get a real job. However, Dewey takes a call intended for Ned, asking him if he is able to fill in for a teacher at the exclusive Horace Green Elementary School. Seeing a chance to acquire some easy money, Dewey impersonates Ned and turns up at Horace Green.

Initially he intends to keep his head down and get through the experience unscathed – his first question to the class being, "I've got a hangover. Who knows what that means?" However, he chances to hear his pupils in their music lesson, and it occurs to him that the sheer range of precocious talent in the class might make for quite a band. He starts a new class project called "Rock Band," transfers all of his gear to the classroom, and sets about teaching his students the theory and practical elements necessary to be a fully qualified rocker. A local 'Battle of the Bands' is impending, presenting Dewey with the opportunity to earn some money to repay Ned, trump his ex-band mates and exorcise his bitterness at being ejected. He soon realises, however, that for the repressed kids at the school, his lessons are providing them with an escape and a means of expression.

What makes the film so effective is that it lives and breathes with the spirit of rock 'n' roll at its most invigorating. Behind the gags and the fooling, there is a story about emancipation and creativity, and about the importance of finding your own voice regardless of the confines of your surroundings. It's not only a sweet and charming experience, but it's uplifting and gratifying too, confirming that profit means more than money, and that all art is profitable. It's a message Black was attentive to, and careful to voice in the film. Looking to speak to parents as much as children, he expressed a desire that the older generation would allow their kids to find their own path and experiment with different art forms as much as they chose to. "Don't stifle it like those weirdos who have their kids lives planned out all the way," he commented on www.ctv.com. "You're just doing damage." Of course, Black was always going to be the lynchpin of the movie, and its success or failure would rest on his performance; the quality of the film is a testament to the degree of his development since he first appeared on screen. He sets the tone of the picture perfectly, being at turns ridiculous and sincere, pitiful and inspiring, a caricature and a human; and crucially, he is at all times *believable*. He prevents the film from turning into an ill-conceived farce by toning down the mania of his performance, though he himself partly credits this to Richard Linklater's influence. He remembers that when he was in danger of going over the top, taking the film beyond playfulness and into ridiculousness, Linklater would rein him in and bring him back down to Earth. "Linklater brings reality, honesty, and believeability," says Black. But this reining-in was inevitable given Jack's passion for the subject matter, and this enthusiasm remains palpable, animating the whole film. He comments how "I really like to be intense, and there were lots of good opportunities to be intensely passionate about the rock and the communication of the secret inner meaning of rock." This fervour visibly rubs off on the talented young ensemble cast that Linklater assembled. Their appearances are confident and convincing, and the fact that they all played their own instruments is utterly vital to the credibility of the film. The chemistry between Black and his disciples is no illusion, either; Linklater has said that Black in fact became a kind of older brother figure for the cast, entertaining and inspiring them, but also expressing genuine care and interest in them. He goes so far as to remark that Black has had a big impact on all of the young stars' lives. Reports from the set state he would jam with the budding musicians in between shooting, exchanging tips and riffs. Working with children held no fear for Black, either. He roundly rebuffs W. C. Fields' assertion that one should never work with children or animals lest they steal focus, stating that he has enough "cuteness and intensity" of his own to battle that of the children. But he also claimed that a lot of people around him had reservations about his making a "kids" film, asking him if he was sure it was a sound career move. However, Black had utter conviction in the project, sensing the edge and subversive quality to the film that would make it something truly engaging. He could also see that the film was shaping up to be remarkably funny. What's more, Black even managed to squeeze in a cameo for his buddy Gass – or not, as the case may be. "I heard that I was in *School of Rock*," Gass laughed in *Blender*. His parents were sure they had seen him in a trailer for the film, and were trying to convince him he was in the picture despite his insistence he hadn't shot a single frame. "My mom said, 'You don't think I know my own kid?' My mind was spinning. I'm going, 'Maybe they photoshopped me in as some sort of prank.' Then I saw the trailer, and there's a bald guy with a goatee who looks nothing like me."

The film was premiered on September 24, 2003 in the States, and on general release by October 3. It shot straight to the top of the Box Office, grossing just under $20 million on its opening weekend, and totalling a worldwide gross of over $131 million. Critical response was highly favourable. Writing in *The Chicago Sun Times*, Roger Ebert praised the film's richness of tone, saying "If quirky, independent, grown-up outsider filmmakers set out to make a family movie, this is the kind of movie they would make." *Variety* magazine felt less of the delivery of the film, but noted that "the whole show is basically Black's," saying "with hilarious physical business ... he pretty much single-handedly keeps the formulaic progress funny." Reel.com also praised the vitality of Black's performance, calling him "perfect in the role of the well-meaning, elementary school Svengali as he makes Dewey's zeal for the only subject he knows a vibrant, beautiful thing." A plethora of awards nominations inevitably followed with Black scooping two Teen Choice Awards nominations (one for 'Choice Movie Actor in a Comedy' and one for 'Choice Movie Liar'); he was also nominated for a Golden Globe for 'Best Actor in a Comedy or Musical' (though he lost out to Bill Murray in *Lost in Translation*); and managed to win an MTV Movie Award for 'Best Comedic Performance'. The film was also given another MTV Movie Awards nomination for 'Best On-Screen Team'.

The film's accompanying soundtrack featured original songs written for the film as well as tracks by Cream, The Doors, Iggy And The Stooges, The Ramones and Led Zeppelin. Interestingly, Linklater wanted to use Zeppelin's 'Immigrant Song' for the film, but knew how difficult it was to get the band to agree to license their music for films – he had wanted to use tracks in *Dazed and Confused* (the film is named after the Led Zeppelin song), but had not been able to obtain the rights. For *School of Rock*, he had Jack record a plea to the surviving members of the band in front of 1,000 pleading fans. The plea worked and the rights were indeed obtained to use the song in the film.

* * *

A month after *School of Rock* was premiered, Black also announced that the script for the Tenacious D movie was now complete. Displaying his penchant for self-aggrandising, he told a reporter whilst promoting *School of Rock:* "We have now officially completed the Tenacious D screenplay. It's called *Tenacious D in The Pick of Destiny*. Five years in the making, countless corpses in our wake, we have in our grasp what will certainly come to be known as the greatest document of historical significance since the dawn of time." Since Working Title and Red Hour films had taken over the project, the band had failed to settle on a satisfying script. Despite hiring some top writers, they had struggled to capture Jack and Gass' humour effectively, and forced the pair into writing the script themselves. For five years they had sat on the concept, but in the space of three weeks, the final script was both started in earnest and completed. Lynch remembers that he was the catalyst for the band deciding to write the script themselves, telling Jack: "Nobody can tell you how to be the D. You guys are the D. Let's write it ourselves." They devised a grand total of six treatments, before deciding on the strongest one and refining it into the final outline for the plot. Then for three weeks solid, without a single night out, Black would go round to Lynch's house and stay into the early hours of the morning writing. Gass would appear to contribute his ideas and act as a kind of sounding board for gags and lines. At the end of this intensive period, they had finally completed the script that they had first envisaged at the end of their HBO series. Filming was scheduled to start at the end of 2003, with Lynch at the helm, but before it started Black was to be cast in a project he couldn't bring himself to turn down. It was a casting that would take over his life for the coming months and potentially make or break his career. Like the titular ape of this latest film, the new project would cast a very sizeable shadow over Jack's life and environment … a role in Peter Jackson's *King Kong*.

Chapter 8

A 'FRAT PACK', A WOMAN, AND A 25 FT GORILLA

On November 4, 2003, *Tenacious D: The Complete Masterworks* was released, a DVD of the band performing live at The Brixton Academy in London, as well as all of the band's videos, the complete HBO series, a studio and tour documentary, and some bonus clips from TV performances. The live show demonstrates the Tenacious D live experience in all of its bizarre and hilarious glory, the band performing the hits from their debut, as well as a few songs that didn't make the album plus some exclusive material. But the band's means of promoting the DVD release was just as imaginative as the product itself. They appeared at the launch for the DVD dressed in skin-tight lycra superhero costumes, each with a large "D" on the chest. They declared that they would be staging a hunger strike, suspended in a glass box over the intersection where the MTV studio is located in New York. The hunger strike would last 45 days, and only end before then if one of three conditions was met; if *The Complete Masterworks* went platinum, there came an end to world hunger, or there was peace in the Middle East. "If we need nourishment, we will live off each other's rock," Black quipped – but unfortunately, they were only able to last 45 minutes until their appetites got the better of them. After being pulled into the air, Black began to lose his nerve, and Gass revealed a stash of hidden M&M's in his costume that he frantically devoured. The DVD would go on to sell extremely well, ultimately being certified platinum.

In 2003 Jack also took a role as producer on a documentary entitled *Sixty Spins Around The Sun*, which had been written and directed by his partner, Laura Kightlinger. The film concerns Randy Credico, a comedian who was inspired to political activism when the Rockefeller drug laws were passed in the 1970s. The laws were excessively draconian and rendered the sentence for selling of two ounces of narcotics equivalent to that of Second Degree murder – a minimum of fifteen years in prison. Credico was clearly an inspiration for Kightlinger, who had been talking about him when she and Black first met. "She was obsessed with Randy Credico before we even started going out," Jack remembered in *Democracy Now!* She had been making the documentary since they first started dating, seven years prior to its eventual release. Black was initially drawn to become involved simply because it was a passion project of Laura's, but as he educated himself about the Rockefeller Drug Laws and Credico's mission, he became interested on a personal level. "I wanted to become a part of this project because the Rockefeller laws are just … I think they're insane," he states. Whilst discussing the film with Amy Goodman, a reporter from *Democracy Now!*, Jack also took the opportunity to discuss his political views a little further. Stressing his opposition to the Bush administration, he remarked how "as soon as we started going into Iraq, it just felt so wrong … Now it seems like you're crazy if you're not against this whole campaign, as far as I'm concerned." He also referred to the fact that muscle-man-turned-Hollywood-action-man Arnold Schwarzenegger was now the Governor for California as "scary" saying, "I'm sorry. I apologise to the rest of the country and the rest of the world … None of my friends would vote for Arnold Schwarzenegger and it's kind of shocking when he gets elected." He commented that in Hollywood, there was an atmosphere of tension and fear, and that many felt life in America was going to get worse before it got better. And despite his outspoken stance on the political climate in America, he had no concerns about being targeted or singled out by political forces. "I'm not really out there with my politics, you know, front and centre of my work like Randy was," he said, and as such dismissed any suggestions he might be blacklisted – however, he also remarked that he would not be concerned about being targeted for something he truly believed in.

Black's next and final appearance of 2003 would be on TV, for a cameo in US sitcom *Will and Grace*. Laura Kightlinger had been periodically writing for the show since 2000, and had a small part in the series as a nurse named Sheila. Jack appeared in the sixth season of the show, in the episode 'Nice In White Satin' where he starred as a somewhat unhinged doctor named Isaac Hershberg.

Black's musical endeavours in 2004 included appearing as a guest vocalist on an album by Probot, a Dave Grohl passion-project. Grohl enlisted a staggering roll-call of underground rock and metal alumni to sing on the record, including Max Cavalera of Latin-metallers Sepultura and Soulfly, Lee Dorrian of Birmingham-based Napalm Death, and Lemmy of Motörhead. Black sang on 'I Am The Warlock', a hidden track beginning around nine minutes after the last song. The tune marches along a huge stoner-rock riff, with Black bellowing typically abstract and bizarre lyrics over the top. He delivers a impressively credible performance as a metal vocalist, his roar rumbling and commanding, but it's difficult to listen to Jack sing in such a stylised way and not hear some sort of affectionate parody – even if it is assumed on the listener's part rather than intended on the performer's.

Obviously concerned about the prospect of another four years with President Bush, Tenacious D became proactive in the 2004

Presidential election race. On July 6 they played a benefit at the Henry Fonda Theatre in Los Angeles, in aid of John Kerry, the Democratic opponent to the Republican's George W. Bush. The band played the set with a full band, including Dave Grohl on drums, and a string quartet. Despite pulling out all the stops – the set included covers of Led Zeppelin's 'Good Times, Bad Times' and Dio's 'Holy Diver' – Bush was nonetheless re-elected in November of 2004. When asked about the election, Black was happy to once again speak out about his view on the political situation, telling the *New Zealand Herald* that, "I've felt disappointed in the past about things that our government has done or people who have been elected," he said, "but this is the first time I've felt really ashamed to be part of that country. It's definitely my lowest point ... the worst I've felt about my country." Kyle even managed to put a little bit of the blame for Bush's re-election on Black's shoulders specifically. He remarked that the saddest aspect of Bush's re-election for him personally was that it came down to the state of Ohio, and Tenacious D were originally planning to play benefits for Kerry in Ohio. However, Jack's schedule for the forthcoming *King Kong* movie prevented the pair touring that state. "If you [Jack] hadn't been doing *King Kong*, we might have been able to swing Ohio," he ventures.

Before *King* Kong, however, Jack returned to help his old friend Dan Harmon with Channel 101. He was developing a show called *Laserfart*; managing to trump *Computerman* in terms of sheer weirdness, it sees Dan eating a burrito from a malfunctioning microwave, and subsequently being bestowed with the ability to fart lasers. He adopts the inventive moniker 'Laserfart' and sets about ridding the city of crime. Black starred in the second episode of the show as 'The Elegant Hunter', a leather-clad super villain who decides Laserfart will make for a challenging hunt. The episode helped the show survive a few more episodes before it went the way of *Computerman*.

Jack's next release in the US would be a testament to both the fickle nature of the industry and the double-edged sword of success. In summer 2002, after the release of *Ice Age,* Black had shot a film with Ben Stiller entitled *Envy*. Directed by Barry Levinson, who had also shot 1988's hit *Rain Man*, it was an off-the-wall comedy that saw Black invent a spray that can vaporize faeces. The invention makes him wildly rich, but his neighbour, played by Stiller, is overcome with jealousy as his life spirals downward. The film is, frankly, very poor. The script contains little to no hearty laughs, and Black seems curiously inanimate, not so much restrained as repressed by the lifelessness of the screenplay. The talents of Stiller and Christopher Walken go entirely wasted as well, with neither managing to drag the film above the peculiarly low standard it sets for itself. The film was initially scheduled for release on May 30, 2003, but poor audience reception in test screenings meant that the film was first heavily re-edited. The new cut saw no improvement in audience response, so distributors DreamWorks decided to shelve it, intending it to go straight-to-video. However, Jack's success in *School of Rock* encouraged them to repeal that decision, and on April 30, 2004 the film went on general release. It was a complete flop, grossing well under half of its $40 million budget and proving that having a major star in the ascendancy in a picture is no guarantee of success. It was never released in cinemas in the UK, instead going straight-to-video. During a later press conference for another film, Jack Black publicly apologised for *Envy*, once again displaying his disarming honesty regarding the projects he works on.

* * *

Jack's next movie would be a big success, even if he only had a small cameo in the picture. It is not so much significant in Black's career specifically, but as an indicator of the status of post-Millennium American mainstream comedy. *The Anchorman: The Legend of Ron Burgundy* is undoubtedly the jewel in the collective crown of the so-called Frat Pack, seen by many as the new princes of US comedy. The meteoric rise of the group of actors that came to compose this collection is a tale in itself. The term was first coined in an article written by Susan Wloszczyna in the June, 2004 edition of *USA Today*. It spoke of an "on-going comedy cabal of thirty-something funny guys who can't stop crashing each other's pictures" (though *Entertainment Weekly* had previously dubbed them the somewhat less catchy 'Slacker Pack').

USA Today's article lists Stiller as the "de facto kingpin," alongside Vince Vaughn, Luke and Owen Wilson, Will Ferrell and, of course, Jack Black. But what is so interesting about the group is that despite their constant on-screen interactions, and the dialogue that their films engage in via their own specific vernacular, the actors all come from separate backgrounds and different parts of the States, rising to prominence in relatively distinct circles, albeit in tandem with one another. Jack's version of the Pack's rise to fame is somewhat embellished: "It originated when Ben Stiller called all the top comedians of the time over to his head quarters that he has inside the Hollywood sign," he claimed in *Movie Interview*. "People don't know but he spent a billion dollars to hollow out this huge thing. Tim Robbins works the door and we all have these huge Frat Pack helicopters that come out of the 'O'... We talk about what our plan is to dominate the world of comedy: 'Will, you take the new Christmas movie. Jack, you go rock. Ben, go do a romantic lead, a Jew with anxiety.'" And while this version of events might not be particularly close to the reality of the situation, Stiller was indeed somewhat of a pre-cursor to Black, first receiving major exposure for MTV's *The Ben Stiller Show* before giving Jack his first major leg-up with *The Cable Guy*. This was also the first point of contact between Owen Wilson, Stiller and Black, but Wilson is a Texan native who had first garnered attention in Wes Anderson's indie flick *Bottle Rocket*, a film which he had co-written and starred in alongside his brother, Luke. Wilson and Stiller would go on to become a kind of unofficial double act, starring together in *The Royal Tenenbaums*, *Zoolander* and *Starsky and Hutch*. Vince Vaughn grew up in Minneapolis, and upon moving to Hollywood, began getting roles in big-budget films like *The Lost World: Jurassic Park* and the 1998 remake of *Psycho*. However, it was his appearance in 2003's *Old School* that truly gave him the opportunity to demonstrate his comedic abilities, and since then he has gone on to star alongside Wilson, Stiller and a host of other minor players in the Frat Pack circle. *Old School* was also an important film for another Frat Packer, Will Ferrell, who had been a regular guest on *Saturday Night Live*. The film marked his induction into this extensive band of merry-makers.

And from the convergence of these divergent paths, the circle has continued to widen, now taking in other contemporary American actors such as Steve Carrell and Paul Judd, and filmmakers like Judd Apatow. But *Anchorman: The Legend of Ron Burgundy* is the film that featured the largest number of these actors, both in main and cameo roles, and has since gone on to become the defining work of the Frat Pack phenomenon. The film stars Will Ferrell as the egocentric, narcissistic and superficial anchorman of the title. Alongside him are his news team: field reporter Brian Fantana (played by Paul Judd); sports reporter Champ Kind (played by David Koechner); and weatherman Brick Tamland (played by Steve Carrell). The film begins with the team enjoying the high life, and the Number 1 spot in the ratings. However, they are horrified to discover that a woman has been hired as a field reporter, and further horrified to discover that the woman in question – Veronica Corningstone (played by Christina Applegate) – has aspirations of credible journalism and anchor status. Burgundy falls for Corningstone, however, and the movie charts his attempts to woo her and the inevitable fall-out. Black appears as a leather-clad biker who, disgruntled that Burgundy has thrown a burrito in his face, kicks his faithful canine companion Baxter off a bridge. The film also features Luke Wilson and Vince Vaughn in smaller roles, and cameos from Ben Stiller and Tim Robbins.

It would be wrong to credit the film with a profundity that it neither strives for nor requests. It would also be inaccurate to say that *Anchorman* represents most appropriately the themes and stylistic qualities that Frat Pack films often deal with; it is more surreal, stylised and obtuse than many of the films that can be said to fall into that category. But in another sense, it is the ideal ambassador for the Frat Pack, simply on the grounds that it is completely *hilarious*. It is composed entirely of the very essence of cult status, a never-ending series of set-ups and one liners that seem fundamentally absurd, and yet could not have been delivered by any other character in any other film. Take the scene where Ron is working out in his office, "sculpting the guns"; or a sequence where he parades around the TV station sporting a full erection; Brian Fantana's attempts to seduce Corningstone with a cologne named 'Sex Panther'; and countless other bizarre and uproarious encounters. Critics received the film with seemingly as much bafflement as amusement, but failed to predict the cult status the movie would acquire.

But the question remains, what is distinct about the success of the Frat Pack, and how, if at all, does it relate to Jack Black? Most have focused simply on the actors that feature in a given film, but if this is the case, Jack would not really be considered a part of that group at all. With the exception of *Anchorman: The Legend of Ron Burgundy,* in which he had but a cameo role, he has appeared in none of the movies that would be considered the principal Frat Pack films. By a similar logic, it would be wrong to class the films of Wes Anderson, such as *Bottle Rocket, The Royal Tenenbaums* or *The Darjeeling Limited* as Frat Pack movies, despite the regular appearances of many members of that group – the films share little to no stylistic or thematic similarities with the likes of *Old School, Dodgeball or Starsky and Hutch.* So what is distinct about Frat Pack movies?

The films principally revolve around humour derived from contemporary, Western anxieties, almost always presented from a masculine world-view. The films rely heavily on the tribulations of relationships and sex, but with a particular emphasis on platonic male interactions in relation to sex. This is clearly evidenced in *Anchorman: The Legend of Ron Burgundy*, which is as much about the news team's response to Ron and his dealings with Veronica as it as about Ron and Veronica's relationship specifically. The treatment of this concept varies considerably from film to film. In *Anchorman* it is absurd and inane; in *The Wedding Crashers* it is framed by a sentimental love story; in *The Forty Year Old Virgin* the main character must 'come of age', which necessitates emancipation from his friends. But the draw of the films is always the male characters and their response to sexual liaisons, as well as various other topics of concern such as appearance, work, family, friendship and so on. Of course, not all of the Frat Pack films focus on sex, but beyond this the principal similarities stem from the distinctive personalities and styles of the main actors that compose the Frat Pack. The fact remains that Black has actually appeared in very few of these films, and what might be considered his most important movies – *School of Rock, Shallow Hal, High Fidelity* and so on – are so shot through with the distinctive voices of their respective collaborators, that they stand as quite distinctive from the Frat Pack.

Perhaps the impact of the mass commercialisation of comedy that some attribute to the Frat Pack is actually more important than the loosely tied similarities of each actor and each film. What is clear is that from the end of the 1990s to the current day, comedy became a huge market in mainstream film, perhaps more so than ever before. Perhaps this was simply due to the ever increasing popularity of cinema, perhaps it was a coincidence, perhaps it was fuelled by the Frat Pack. While being labelled a member of the Frat Pack was not a golden ticket to a successful movie, it certainly gave a sense of momentum and did no harm in terms of exposure. This is a fact that has not escaped Jack. While it would be entirely ill informed to refer to him riding the crest of a wave, he knows the Frat Pack phenomenon has done his career no harm. Perhaps because of his comparative distance to the group, he never took on the sense of resentment that some other members have for the moniker. "I love it!" he remarked. "All of them I think would like to destroy that thing, but I love it. I think those guys are great and I'm in there? Yeah! I'm the only card-carrying member that actually shows up for

Frat Pack meetings!" What has made Jack so distinct in this group is that he is able to dabble with the style, appearing alongside Ben Stiller in *Envy* or Will Ferrell in *Anchorman*, but also return to more distinct projects, such as the ones he would move onto, with the likes of Jared Hess or Michel Gondry.

Next Jack moved onto another CGI film, but this time he had secured a leading role amongst a stellar cast of talent. *Shark Tale* is an underwater caper, the story of Oscar, played by Will Smith, a fish who owes a lot of money to loan sharks. He is due to be bumped off, but a chance encounter with Jack Black's benevolent, vegetarian shark Lenny affords him an interesting opportunity. Lenny is resisting his father, a Mob boss played by Robert De Niro, who insists Lenny must become a cold-blooded killer like the rest of the gang. As such, Oscar and Lenny shack up together, with Oscar perpetuating the myth that he has previously killed a shark in combat. Oscar's new found fame attracts the attention of the superficial, self-absorbed Lola (played by Angelina Jolie), much to the dismay of his true paramour Angie (Renée Zellweger).

The film did not capture many critic's imaginations. Since the CGI Boom in the late 1990s the formula had been wearing thin, and a fully computer animated film was no longer a spectacle that would draw audiences on its own merit. Further to this, for many the film squandered the quite astounding cast it had assembled; it is certainly funny in parts, but the plot is too convoluted, and for a film aimed at children and families, references to the Mafia, loan sharks and love triangles seems a bit over-ambitious. Another ocean based CGI film, *Finding Nemo*, had been released just a year previously, to widespread audience and critical acclaim. *Shark Tale* just didn't measure up in inventiveness or laughs. The film even attracted some criticism for its potentially negative perpetuation of Italian-American stereotypes, with all the Mafioso sharks sporting a predictably 'wise guy' accent. Black's character Lenny was also the subject of some suspicion. Many critics, including a reviewer for *Premiere,* picked up on the thinly-veiled gay sub-text of the film – a shark who espouses masculine standards of worth, is ashamed to admit he's vegetarian, and subsequently emotionally withdraws from his over-bearing, macho father-figure. This even prompted the American Family Association to publish an article entitled "Something's Swishy About *Shark Tale*", which instead of applauding the film for its forward-thinking and tolerance, implied the film was inappropriate for children. "*Shark Tale* comes far too close to taking a bite out of traditional moral and spiritual values," wrote Ed Vitagliano of the American Family Association Online in 2004.

Such concerns didn't affect sales of the film, however, and it was a huge success at the box office. It managed to gross almost $370 million worldwide, a colossal sum even by Hollywood's standards. Predictably, the press were far more interested in hearing about Black's impending role in *King Kong* than *Shark Tale*, as news had since broke that he would be starring as Carl Denham in Peter Jackson's first post-*Lord of the Rings* movie. *Shark Tale* premiered on September 10, 2004 at the Venice Film Festival, and a short time later, Jack got the chance to revisit the famous Cannes Film Festival for a showing of the movie. Making a spectacular entrance astride a giant inflatable shark, he told a reporter from *ET Online*: "This is my second time, I was here twelve years ago with a little film called *Bob Roberts.* This is totally different though, 'cos this time I'm doing interviews and stuff. Nobody cared that I was here last time." In fact, as mentioned last time he had not even been invited, merely using his dad's residence in Cannes as a veil for turning up.

Jack's last appearance of 2004 was with Tenacious D in *Tom Goes to the Mayor*, a new cartoon airing on the Cartoon Network's 'Adult Swim', a late-night line-up aimed at a mature audience. Bob Odendirk was on board as the show's executive producer, no doubt instrumental in setting up the duo's cameo. The animation follows Tom and his proposals to the Mayor of fictional Jefferton. A bizarre and closeted individual, he takes Tom's proposals and transforms them into something completely different. Jack and Kyle appear in 'Bear Traps', an episode that sees Tom and the Mayor decide that surrounding play areas with bear traps is the only means of adequately protecting Jefferton's children. They star as bear trap manufacturers, and after the proposal fails to convince the town's council, Tom and the Mayor cast them in a musical production that preaches the benefits of bear traps.

2005 was a comparatively quiet year professionally for Jack, as the filming for *King Kong* went up a gear. However, it was also a tumultuous time privately as by early that year Jack and his partner of eight years, Laura Kightlinger, split up. Jack had always been relatively reticent to speak about his personal life, choosing to keep it private and not have it lived out in the public arena. But regardless of the circumstances surrounding their break-up, what is clear is that in early 2005 Jack had moved out of the house they shared together, and was living in the Four Seasons Hotel in Los Angeles while he waited for his new house to be prepared.

In April of that difficult year, Tenacious D were asked to play a set at the surprise 40th Birthday Party of Frank Black – aside from being Jack's namesake, Frank Black had achieved international renown as the singer and principal songwriter for the mid-1980s to early-1990s alternative rock band The Pixies, a group that Nirvana frontman Kurt Cobain once identified as a main influence. The band are frequently acknowledged as the forerunners to the alternative rock explosion that dominated the early 1990s, with bands from the Smashing Pumpkins to Sonic Youth all owing an obvious debt to The Pixies. By 1993 they had disbanded, however, and Frank had continued his career with Frank Black And The Catholics. In 2004, The Pixies had reformed, headlining the UK's Reading and Leeds festivals amongst various others.

It was while at this party that Black (Jack, not Frank) met Tanya Haden – or rather, met her again. She was the daughter of renowned jazz double bass player Charlie Haden, who during the 1960s and 1970s become one of the most respected double bass players working; he went on to lead the Liberation Music Orchestra, an experimental, political jazz outfit. The father of triplet girls, Charlie's musicality clearly rubbed off on his children, with all of his brood exceptionally talented. Tanya is an accomplished cellist and singer, her sister Rachel a bass player, and her other sister Petra a violinist and vocalist. Petra and Rachel formed the alternative rock band 'that dog.' (sic) in 1991, which dissolved in 1997; perhaps the best known of all of Charlie's children, Petra has also performed with the likes of Foo Fighters, Green Day, Weezer and The Decembrists. The three triplets had also performed together as The Haden Triplets, and Charlie's son Josh was also the bassist and singer for the recently split Spain. In a further chance connection, former that dog. vocalist Anna Waronker had married Steve McDonald, who played bass on Tenacious D's debut album.

Born in New York on October 11, 1971, Tanya had first met Jack at the Crossroads School in Santa Monica. Jack remembers her well from this time: "I had a crush on her. But we weren't, like, close buddies. She was too pretty, and I was scared to talk to her." A party roughly twenty years later was probably not the ideal venue for a reunion either, as Jack had previously expressed discomfort with this scenario; he had stated that he gets uncomfortable around people he doesn't know, and its fairly inevitable he'll meet some at a party. On this occasion, however, he did not allow Tanya Haden's attractiveness or the wealth of people he didn't know to stop him talking to her. Affirming that "I would never have dated her in High School," he recounted hilariously on *The David Letterman Show* that, "I had the courage … I'd never had the courage before but then I thought, 'Wait a second, I'm a world-renowned movie-star, I can do it!' It's a shame that that's what it took. I recommend it to people who have low self-esteem. Become a movie star of world renown." And Jack's courage obviously payed off; the pair struck up a rapport and kept in touch.

Jack next made a brief cameo appearance in the pilot of *Awesometown*, commissioned by Fox and made by an LA-based group of filmmakers called the Lonely Island. Jack introduced the show, claiming to be George Washington and telling viewers that "the show you're about to see is *Awesometown*, and it's the funniest thing since sliced bread, which I invented." Unfortunately, Fox did not agree – Jack's intro was the funniest part of the entire pilot, and the show was not picked up for development.

Before the long-awaited release of *King Kong*, Jack had just enough time to perform in one more benefit with Tenacious D. In late August of 2005, Hurricane Katrina had struck America, causing widespread damage, the most severe of which was localised around New Orleans, Louisiana. On September 22, Tenacious D played at the Wiltern Theatre in LA to help raise funds for the relief effort.

* * *

On December 5, 2005 – finally – the film that Black had been working on since 2003 hit cinemas: *King Kong*. Jack clearly remembers his motives for taking the role. He later agreed that his part and the entire script were well written and devised, regardless of the director in charge, but Black actually read neither before accepting the role. He took the part on the strength of Peter Jackson's position as director. In fact, he had been hassling his agent to get in touch with Jackson for quite some time, as he told Daniel Robert Epstein of *Suicide Girls*. "I talked to my agent a few months beforehand and said, 'God, I want to be in a Peter Jackson movie, can't you make it happen? You're a power agent.' She was like, 'Dude, everybody wants to be in a Peter Jackson movie.'"

His agent wasn't wrong. Peter Jackson had started as an independent director in his native New Zealand, directing low-budget splatter-horror films such as *Bad Taste* and *Braindead*. Entirely self-taught and with no formal training in film, the home-made special effects and imagination of these films marked him out as a distinctive new voice. In 1994, he released *Heavenly Creatures* to widespread critical acclaim, and his career really took off. By 1997 he had won the rights to J. R. R. Tolkien's classic fantasy epic *The Lord of the Rings*, and taking the roles of director, co-producer and co-writer, set about shooting the most talked about project of the 21st Century, and arguably the most successful trilogy of all-time. The three films had a collective budget of $280 million, but more than justified this huge amount with an estimated gross revenue of $2.91 billion, thirty Oscar nominations, and seventeen wins. They are widely seen as landmark films in Hollywood history.

However, the challenge of adapting a book previously thought by many to be un-filmable was clearly not enough for Jackson. His next project was announced as a remake of 1933's *King Kong*, the film that had first ignited his passion for cinema and inspired him to become a director. "The original Kong is just a wonderful piece of escapist entertainment," he remarked on www.darkhorizons.com. "It also has this wonderful heart and soul, with the emphatic creature who, when I was nine, made me cry when he was killed on the Empire State Building."

The journey from conception to release of Peter Jackson's *King Kong* was long and arduous. In 1996 a version of the film was in development, with a script completed, but later cancelled by the studio; prior to the shooting of *Lord of the Rings* some initial designs were completed; and then during the production of *Lord of the Rings: The Two Towers*, Jackson was contacted and asked to direct a re-make. He was reportedly paid $20 million for his involvement, the highest fee ever offered to a Hollywood director. Given his success with *Lord of the Rings*, this came as no surprise.

And so, we return to Jack hassling his agent when news of the re-make first broke, desperately hoping for some involvement in the project. Sure enough, Jackson had been interested in Black, and actually got in touch personally, calling Black and asking him to interview for a role in the film. "I would have come and interviewed for 'Carrots on Ice' if he was directing it," Black remarked, but the role was in fact far more stimulating than that. Jackson was clearly impressed with Black as well, as he cast him in the role of Carl Denham, one of the film's key characters. "He's a smart and versatile actor blessed with an abundance of energy and charm," Jackson stated, though Black had not always been his first choice for the role. For his original 1996 version of the film, he had stated that "I was hoping we could get George Clooney or Robert De Niro." Stiff competition indeed, and Jack was understandably delighted to have got the part. He has always picked his roles based on the credentials of those involved with the project, and Peter Jackson was a director who had proved himself one of the most esteemed in cinema. What's more, Black looked for directors he could get along with on a personal level, as he would have to spend a large part of his life in their company. Jackson fit that brief, too.

Black's role was as Carl Denham, a film-maker who has fallen on hard times. Desperate to pay off some long-standing debts and make his name, he resolves to shoot a picture on the uncharted Skull Island, and thus leads an ill-fated expedition there. Travelling with a young starlet named Ann (Naomi Watts), and screenwriter Jack (Adrien Brody), the pioneers soon discover that the inhabitants of Skull Island are not used to entertaining visitors. Beyond the vicious and bloodthirsty natives, the island is populated by dinosaurs and other monstrous creatures, including a 25-foot gorilla that is revered as a god. The crew make hasty preparations to leave, but they soon discover that Ann has been abducted to be sacrificed to Kong, and Jack/Denham declares his intentions to rescue her. This is more than suited to Denham, who sees Kong as his chance to chase away his demons and fix his place in the history books forever.

Black recalls that at the time of casting, Jackson would often give Orson Welles as a point of reference for the character of Denham. Welles was a legendary actor and director throughout the mid-20th Century, most famously co-writing, producing, directing and playing the lead in 1941's highly celebrated *Citizen Kane*. Despite Welles' intimidating stature and repute, it was at least a reference Black could get to grips with, and had a large influence of his portrayal of Denham. Black watched all of Orson Welles' films to develop his own character, focusing in on his arrogance and ambition, though he notes that Orson also had talent to back these character traits up where Denham does not.

More of a challenge for Black were the extended CGI action scenes in the film, especially considering he had not been in an action film since *Demolition Man*, and at that time there was not much pressure on his performance. He decided to prepare himself both physically and mentally by visiting his old college, and states that he did a fair amount of training to prepare for shooting. He would go down to his old university, UCLA, where he knew of a field that went largely unused. As an alumnus he felt entitled to make the most of the facilities, and as such would visit the field to practise scenes and scenarios. He would pretend to be chased by some of the creatures that inhabit Skull Island, careering around the field and summoning the fear and adrenaline of the situation. There must have been some use to the training, because Jack claims that acting with special effects for the first time was no major issue for him. "I felt like I was born to do it," he claims, remarking that as an actor "pretending that something's happening that's not really happening" is the point anyway. Indeed, with his almost child-like enthusiasm and verve, the opportunity to let loose and run as fast as he could, screaming as loud as he dared, was something he relished. "I feel like I am ready to be in extreme death-defying situations now," he ventured to Daniel Robert Epstein. It was a method so successful, he claims, he intends to pass it on to a younger generation of acting talent: "I'm gonna start a class, an actor's studio called 'Running Around In A Green Field'. It's the Jables method."

While Black's Denham contains much of the heady energy that has defined his on-screen career, he was not daunted by the prospect of playing such a big non-comedic role. The chance to do something he had not done before had always motivated Black, and he referred to the dark and menacing tone of the film as "a cool change of pace."

Fully primed to tackle the role, Jack discovered that the atmosphere on set was not quite what he had been expecting. He was fully aware of the reports of amity and fellowship from the *Lord of the Rings* set, of the cast members making enduring friendships and embarking on real-life adventures to match those portrayed in the film. Jack felt a pressure to feel the same for his cast mates and continue in the vein that the *LOTR* crew had established. While he asserts that the actors' enjoyed one another's company on set, they never achieved the level of camaraderie that the *Lord of the Rings* set had been famous for. "It wasn't a lovefest with all the actor's in this movie," he states, "because the movie has some real fucking dark things to it. Maybe it wasn't supposed to be that kind of summer-camp vibe." With the film being shot in New Zealand, he even remembers seeing testimony to the *Lord of the Rings* legacy, such as graffiti: on his walk to the set every day, he would pass a wall with "Frodo was here" scrawled on it, no doubt increasing the sense of pressure Black felt to match the fraternity of Jackson's previous cast.

There was some fun on set, however. He revealed that Jackson taught him to use some of the old film equipment that features in the film, and that he used it to shoot some mini-films of his own (in a foreshadowing of his role in 2008's *Be Kind Rewind*). As a collector of items and artefacts from Hollywood's illustrious history, Jackson even had one of the cameras that the original *King Kong* movie was shot with. "Me and the other people who were on the film within the film learned how to load and shoot movies with it," Jack revealed to *Suicide Girls*. "We actually shot some really dumb movies in preparation. I think they might be one of the DVD extras. In fact, they'd better be, because we put a lot of thought into those turdy little movies." Jack also found other ways to unwind, including one notorious incident that he revealed in an interview with *GQ* in January 2006. Explaining how his first full year of non-smoking as an adult came to an abrupt end, he recalls a "lost weekend" during the filming of *King Kong*. Despite asserting that normally he is a very responsible and understated figure on set, on one occasion he had some spare time to kill during a break in his schedule. On this occasion he decided to take some ecstasy with another cast member (whose name he did not reveal), and went on what amounts to a rampage. "Just running around, dancing around, drinking and ecstasising," he told Chris Heath for *GQ* (although the interviewer was never quite certain that Black wasn't just fictionalizing for fun). The most unfortunate outcome of the foray was that Black began smoking again.

King Kong was always going to be a difficult prospect. Peter Jackson not only chose to re-make one of the most iconic and memorable films in cinema history, but he also chose to do it immediately after his *Lord of the Rings* trilogy, a series of films almost impossible to trump in spectacle and grandeur. However, he just about manages it. The action set-pieces mark the film as the natural predecessor of the 1933 original; whilst in the 1930s, a stop-motion animated Kong atop a scale Empire State Building was sufficiently novel to inspire wonder in an audience, the 21st Century cinema-goer requires something considerably more emphatic. With this in mind, Jackson includes a dinosaur stampede, a giant insect pit, a swarm of man-sized bats and a four-way brawl between King Kong and three Tyrannosaurus Rex-type creatures, not to mention the famous city-rampage finale. In terms of sheer ambition and vision, *King Kong* is an absolute triumph, a movie so outrageous and bold you cannot fail to be taken in.

Jack's performance is undoubtedly a success, and prior to its release, it seemed like nobody ever doubted it would be. Considering his lack of experience with pictures of this type, there were remarkably few nay-sayers claiming that Black would not be able to provide the gravitas or depth required for the role. Black's Denham is a fascinating figure; like the egomaniacal conquistador in Herzog's *Aguirre, The Wrath of God*, he is a man who will travel to the heart of darkness to realise his dreams, a man utterly controlled by his obsessive, hubristic nature. And Jack was clear from the start that this was the direction he wanted to take the part in. "[He's] trying to find the sensational niche to carve out for his career," said Black on www.EW.com. "I feel like they cast me in this because I could bring the passion for this character, like he's almost insane with enthusiasm for this quest." Unlike Kinski's Aguirre, however, Black invests Denham with just enough humanity and rationality to keep him from turning into an outright villain, more a figure of misplaced zeal than of intentional evil. Denham is still allowed the final line of the film, the acknowledgement of the humanity within the animal he entrapped, the partial admission of empathy; "Oh no, it wasn't the airplanes. It was beauty killed the beast." Ironically, Jack was not supposed to speak these lines in the remake; Jackson had set them apart for a cameo for the original's star, Fay Wray. However, she passed away before having a chance to shoot the scene, and the most famous words of *King Kong* remained within Denham's cinematic lineage.

Despite all this, however, there is a lingering sense of style over substance, technology over technique, and when $207 million is spent on a film (the budget escalated from $150 million, making it the most expensive single movie ever made at the time), it needs to deliver more than simply spectacle. At over three hours long, Jackson makes the error of thinking that for a film to be epic, it needs to have an epic running time, and so the film drags in its first act and only manages to pick up serious momentum about an hour in. Similarly, the emotional lynchpin of the film – Kong and Ann's connection, whatever that may be – simply seems overdone, an incongruous and artless counterpoint to the adrenaline-fuelled thrills that the rest of the film offers. And while the CGI *is* some of the most technically adept to have been witnessed in film, it is no longer enough to keep a film buoyant without the aid of a well told, pacey story. *King Kong* is not a bad film – far from it, in fact – but when a project is so eagerly anticipated, promising so much by virtue of its cast, crew, vision and heritage, it would need to be nigh-on perfect to silence every critic. Unfortunately, *King Kong* is far from perfect.

Critical reception was generally favourable, however. Peter Bradshaw, writing for *The Guardian*, made the bold claim that "everything the 1933 movie has, Jackson has – to the power of a hundred." Carina Chocano noted in *The Los Angeles Times* that the film works as "a travelogue through popular movie genres," passing from "socially conscious drama to comedy, romance, horror, adventure, science-fiction fantasy and doomed love story, cleverly quoting the styles and tropes to which we've become accustomed along the way." Peter Arendt, however, saw this movement as "spectacular, clumsy, hilarious, ludicrously self-indulgent, terrifying and far too long," best summing up the variety of response that the film inspires. Interestingly, the film had a slow start at the box office, no doubt giving some of the investors at Universal Studios a serious fright and some sleepless nights. Fox News declared it a "catastrophe in the making", pointing out that it taken under $10 million on its opening day, and just over $6 million on its second. It was a scenario Jack had been dreading, declaring that so much was riding on the film financially and personally, it would be inconceivable for it to flop. Fortunately, come the following weeks, the film finally took off and eventually grossed an impressive $550 million worldwide by the time it was pulled from cinemas. DVD sales of the film were also very high, contributing to the final $700-million-plus total that has made *King Kong* the fourth most successful movie in Universal Pictures history. If *High Fidelity* had announced Black's arrival, it was *King Kong* that announced his intention to stay.

Chapter 9

JACK BLACK: HUSBAND, FATHER, LUCHA LIBRE

With the monumental success of *King Kong* behind him, Jack also found new happiness in his love life. Since first meeting Tanya at Frank Black's 40th birthday party, their relationship had developed and they had begun dating. Cryptically referring to Tanya in an interview after the release of *King Kong*, he told Chris Heath of *GQ*: "I'm really pissed off, because I just started going out with this girl – I obsessively compulse over things, and she's the centre of my obsessive-compulsive energy vortex of pain right now." His plan to win Tanya round involved burning her a mix CD of his favourite songs. He had assembled a winning hit list of tunes for Tanya, including the likes of Neil Young and Radiohead, but was unable to burn the downloaded songs from iTunes. "It's fucking making me so mad," he ranted. "The technology is fucking me. All I know is that I'm not going to fucking win the heart of the fair maiden because of fucking iTunes." And while this crisis meant that he had to purchase all of the CDs containing the relevant songs, at least his and Tanya's relationship had taken a considerable step forward since he found the courage to talk to her a few months earlier.

In fact, Tanya was to take up quite a lot of Jack's time in the early part of 2006. First, he found the time to make a brief appearance in WWE Velocity, appearing as Ignacio to promote his forthcoming film *Nacho Libre*. He also appeared as himself in Andy Dick's film *Danny Roane: First Time Director*. Black had befriended Dick after they starred together in various projects, including *The Cable Guy* and *Bongwater*. *Danny Roane: First Time Director*, a mockumentary about a troubled actor's debut as a director, also marked Dick's debut feature film. But behind the scenes, something huge was occurring in Jack's life. Unbeknownst to the press, Tanya Haden was pregnant with Jack's baby. On March 14, they shocked everyone by eloping together and getting married, exchanging vows in a private ceremony in Big Sur, California. They had become engaged on the set of *Nacho Libre*, Jack's next feature. The signs were perhaps evident – Black had told a reporter he was "crazy about her" – but he nonetheless attributed her accepting his proposal to the magnetism of the moustache he had to grow for the film. It was just eleven months after the pair had met and a few more since Black and Kightlinger had split. However, given Jack's tendency to keep his private life exactly that, it is not so surprising that he did not inform the world's media of his impending marriage. In 2004 he had briefly discussed his relationship with Laura Kightlinger, expressing his misgivings about the formalities of marriage, describing himself as a cynic about the whole institution. The prospect of making a relationship official, with legal documents and a ceremony, and the obligation for friends to attend with gifts, was not something Black saw as at all appealing. In fact, he had even told Daniel Handler of *The Believer*, he would make a point of keeping it small: "I think if I ever get married I think only twelve people will be invited. Then everyone will be mad. No one's invited. It's just a good old-fashioned elope." While Haden had clearly dissipated his cynicism regarding marriage, he stayed true to his earlier promise and engineered a "good old-fashioned elope." Tanya's jazz musician father Charlie was delighted nonetheless, declaring, "They love each other very much. We're thrilled." Jack still felt it necessary to impress Charlie, however, and admits to having watched all ten hours of Ken Burn's documentary *Jazz* in an attempt to have more common ground with his new father-in-law. His efforts would later be rewarded, though, when in 2008 Haden would invite Black to sing on his new release *Ramblin' Boy*.

Despite the flurry of activity in his home life, Jack had managed to maintain his professional momentum and keep on working. Since September 2005, he had been filming *Nacho Libre*, which was due for release on June 16, 2006. The project had first come about when a producer at Nickelodeon Movies had heard the story of Fray Tormenta, or Friar Storm: a Mexican Priest whom, in order to support the orphanage where he worked, led a secret career in *lucha libre*. Literally meaning 'free fight', *lucha libre* is the art of Mexican wrestling, famous for its combatants donning colourful and distinctive masks of which forcible removal in the ring is the greatest dishonour. Fray Tormenta was himself inspired by two Mexican films: 1963's *El Senor Tormenta* and *Tormenta En El Ring*, so *Nacho Libre* was in fact tapping into a rich vein of Mexican cultural legend. The producer in question, eager to see the story re-told for a modern, English-speaking audience, optimistically approached Jared Hess to direct.

Hess had turned down every picture he had been offered since the runaway success of his debut film, *Napoleon Dynamite*. Eccentric, offbeat and shot for a meagre $400,000, its depiction of a geeky, withdrawn high schooler had struck a chord with comedy fans the world over. Garnering a huge cult following, it marked the arrival of a fiercely distinctive new voice in cinema and grossed an impressive $44.5 million, over one hundred times more than its production cost. However, Hess had since kept his head down, despite the innumerable offers to direct that flooded his way.

However, Nickelodeon's concept immediately appealed to Jared, who had always harboured a fascination with *lucha libre*. Jack remembers that his proactive approach helped spur the film into being. Since seeing *Napoleon Dynamite* Black had set his sights on Hess as the next man he wanted to work with. With this in mind, Black and Mike White – who had recently set up a production company named, of course, 'Black And White' together – got in touch with Jared Hess to express their interest. Hess had also been a fan of *School of Rock*, and to be approached by White and Black with the offer of collaboration must have been too tempting to resist. Hess pitched the concept to Black, who simply replied, "Well, if you're at the helm, my friend, I will go with you."

The film is the story of Ignacio (Black), a friar who acts as the cook in an orphanage he was himself raised in. Due to the lack of adequate funds, the children are forced to eat scraps and leftovers, and Ignacio is roundly derided for his incompetence in the kitchen. One day, whilst collecting day old potato chips to bolster the monastery's meals, he is set upon by a thief and has the chips stolen. Deciding that he and the orphans deserve better, he resolves to stop repressing his wrestling ambitions and transform himself into a Luchador. He teams up with chip thief Steven (Hector Jiminez) and spectacularly loses in his first ever fight. To his surprise, however, he is paid anyway; giving the orphans a fresh green salad the next day, he decides to continue wrestling, also hoping it will aid him in winning the heart of the beautiful Sister Encarnacion. However, wrestling is forbidden by his faith, and he is forced to keep his identity secret and endure the contempt of the other friars. Black And White Productions, along with writer/director Jared Hess and co-writer Jerusha, decided to take a bold approach to the film. It was to be shot entirely on location in Oaxaca, Mexico, using a Mexican, largely non-English speaking crew, and principally Mexican actors. Despite the risks, they had resolved to make the film as authentic as possible, and it was a decision no one regretted. Hess described working with the crew as one of the best experiences he had ever had, declaring his intent to return to Mexico to make another film. Black was also delighted with the striking nature of Oaxaca's landscape. "We got some of the best locations," he remarked, and also stated that he believed far more American directors would be heading to shoot in the stunning locations available. What's more, he reported that the people on the street were delighted to welcome a film crew into their town, but even all this wasn't the full extent of the benefits of shooting on location in Mexico. "I know that the restaurant that I went to every night was stoked that I was there," he claims. "I plucked down a lot of pesos for the various delicious dishes."

It wasn't all beautiful locations and delicious food, however. The various fight sequences in the film required a level of physical dedication from Black that he had not yet encountered in his career. It was vital to the success of the film, despite its comic tone, that the wrestling sequences looked professional and convincing, and this meant training. A genuine Luchador was hired to get Black into shape and comfortable with the basics of wrestling, and Tom – as he was called – told Black that he was a natural talent. Black is not completely oblivious to the fact that Tom may have been merely trying to boost his confidence, but all the same, it worked. However, despite Black's quickly developing skill in the ring, Tom did not once remove his mask and reveal his identity to Black.

The training was also dangerous – during one sequence Black would dive into the audience, only to catch his face on the corner of a metal chair. The gaping wound just above his eye would require many stitches, but Black remained stoical about the decision to perform most of his own stunts. Other challenges included the South American accent that Black had to maintain throughout the film, a facet of the character that also required some preparation. He had to work for many weeks becoming confident enough to improvise in an unnatural accent, and so resolved to spend as much time conversing with Mexican people and learning Spanish as he could spare. Living in Oaxaca for the duration of filming was a great help in this respect.

Despite the challenges that the film presented, Black states that the atmosphere on set was fun and light-hearted. The wrestlers Nacho faces in the film were all professional Luchadors, and despite Black's reservations, they turned out to be "sweethearts." "I was really worried going into it," he revealed to Paul Fischer of *Dark Horizons*, thinking: "*They're gonna break my neck because I'm a sweet, delicate Hollywood comedian. I can't deal with this real athleticism.* But it turned out that I was kick ass and there was nothing to worry about."

Nacho Libre not only marks Jack's debut as a wrestler, but also his debut as a credited producer with 'Black And White', an extra responsibility that he conversely found liberating. Without an executive or higher echelon of authority monitoring the production, Black, Hess and White could be entirely in control, free to explore whichever route they chose. "I think we were good producers," Jack stated in *Cinemablend*. "It's just you have to be filled with opinions ... You really have to think about every aspect of the movie and weigh in and oversee other people's stuff." He also stated that he found the transition from actor to producer a lot smoother than might be imagined. Before he had a role as producer, he was still eager to involve himself with the creative processes on set, voicing his opinions to directors and other crew members about what direction he thought scenes should go in. The only difference now was that it was an obligation rather than a privilege to sound those opinions, as without a strong controlling figure, any movie set would lack direction and focus. One thing Jack was not used to, however, was all the other ground work that comes with a credit as producer – hiring crew members, arranging schedules, organising promotion, liaising with the studio and so on. Nonetheless, this was another aspect that he found both enlightening and enjoyable, and Jack was now in a position to have more control over his career than ever (it also provided a crucial opportunity for Black to hone his producing skills before he started shooting his next and most personal project, *Tenacious D in The Pick of Destiny*).

Nacho Libre is undoubtedly a Jared Hess film; in just two movies he has carved out a niche for himself almost irresistibly distinctive. From the bold, rich colouration of the visuals, to the simple, sparse script and roll-call of naive yet kind-hearted misfits, *Nacho Libre* recalls his debut effort *Napoleon Dynamite* most emphatically. With that said, he also manages to make it distinct enough to stand on its own, to not exist as a mere diluted re-hash of a tremendously unique original. Unfortunately, neither of these statements guarantee the film's quality.

Ultimately, *Nacho Libre* is subject to exactly the same condition as *Napoleon Dynamite*. The film's humour is insistently off-centre, and if it is not to your taste, the whole production will seem lifeless and wilfully obtuse, a bizarre series of half-delivered gags and curiously childish slapstick. If the film's specific vernacular is familiar to you, however, the film will likely be a far more enjoyable and fathomable experience. But ultimately, the film does not have quite the same magical quality as *Napoleon Dynamite*. On paper it should have been a triumph; between them, White, Black and Hess are the principal exponents of American cinema's alt-mainstream comedy stock. They even managed to get legendary film composer Danny Elfman to provide a spirited, wonderfully evocative score to the film. But there is a sense that in adding there has somewhere been a subtraction; that between the Hollywood A-lister and the extra $24.6 million in budget, the single-minded spirit that made *Napoleon Dynamite* feel like such a precious oddity had been lost. It's not that Black's performance isn't very funny. His brings all of his distinctive comedy traits to bear – the spry physicality, the acutely expressive facial contortions, the outrageously demonstrative articulation of lines – but even he can't stop the film feeling less than the sum of its parts. It will certainly rouse more than a few giggles, but despite the profound peculiarity of the film, it is also curiously pallid and forgettable.

Critical response was predictably polarised. Roger Ebert in *The Chicago-Sun Times* remarked that "Jack Black is essentially, intrinsically and instinctively a funny actor," before going on to comment that "it takes some doing to make a Jack Black comedy that doesn't work. But *Nacho Libre* does it." *Rolling Stone* regarded it a "fitfully funny farce", whereas Peter Bradshaw from *The Guardian* called the film "the helium of pure comedy … yours to inhale."

Overall the film ended up on the less favourable end of the critical scale, but this didn't stop it being a major success. It grossed fractionally under $100 million worldwide, doubling that of *Napoleon Dynamite* and comfortably justifying its $25 million budget. By this stage, Jack's star power could make all but the most listless picture a financially bankable prospect. Similarly, the film received a lot of attention from smaller awards bodies. Jack was nominated for a Blimp award, an MTV Movie Award, and no less than four Teen Choice Awards, though he did not win any of them.

During the making of *Nacho Libre*, not only had Tanya and Jack got engaged, but they had also revealed that news about Tanya's pregnancy. Tom Cruise and Brad Pitt had recently become new fathers, and Black was not entirely happy about them stealing the limelight. "A lot of celebrity daddies all of a sudden," he noted, "and I just want to say that I called it first and everybody else just got busy. But I called it like two years ago – 'I wanna have a kid.' And then everybody was like, 'What? Jack's having a kid?' And I'm pretty pissed." In typical Jack Black style, however, this mock petulance was in fact a diversion, luring attention away from the fact that Black wanted the birth of his first child to go relatively unwatched by the media. And with equally typical nonchalance, he revealed at the *Nacho Libre* premiere that his son had in fact been born three days previously, on June 10, 2006. Named Samuel Jason Black, or Sammy, he was born at the Cedars-Sinai Medical Centre in Los Angeles, and Black couldn't contain his excitement at his first time stepping out since the birth. "I've got the babe back home safe and sound," he revealed to Stephen

Silverman at the premiere, "and I'm actually very anxious to get back to my lovin's." His initial thoughts on the long stretch of fatherhood ahead of him were simple: "I think I will be good when it comes to playtime. I don't know how good I'll do with the discipline."

Chapter 10

THE PICK OF DESTINY

Immediately after the release of *Nacho Libre*, Jack took the time to appear in another music video. This time it was the turn of the Eagles Of Death Metal, a band featuring Queens of the Stone Age's Josh Homme. The video to their next single, 'I Want You So Hard (Boy's Bad News)', was to be directed by Akiva Schaffer, one of the three stars of *Awesometown* (the comedy sketch show for which Jack appeared in the pilot). Dave Grohl was already on board to cameo in the video, and due to the involvement of Akiva, Black also agreed to appear. He stars as a bartender who is quite literally blown away by the power of the Eagles Of Death Metal's rock – when confronted by guitar-toting front man Jesse Hughes' riffs, his clothes and wig are completely ripped from his body. As is often the case with special effects, it took quite a few takes for the shot to go just right, which caused much mirth on set.

Music videos aside, 2006 in fact saw the arrival of two babies for Jack. The first – Sammy – may have been dearer to him, but the second was longer in the making and harder work to produce. Lynch and Black had finished the script for *Tenacious D in The Pick of Destiny* in late 2003, but the production of *King Kong* had delayed it being shot. The hold-up might have been a blessing in disguise – Jack was well aware that the first planned release of the film would have it coinciding with the release of *Star Wars Episode III*, *The Matrix Revolutions*, *Harry Potter and the Chamber of Secrets* and *Lord of the Rings: the Two Towers* (though Jack was insistent that no one would bother to go and see those films after the release of *The Pick of Destiny* anyway). It took until April 2005 for the duo to begin work on the film they had first envisaged since their HBO series ended way back in 2000.

The tone of the script was simple: it was Jack's chance to show the world what he personally felt was funny. "I've been in a lot of comedies," he noted to *Suicide Girls*, "and nothing makes me laugh as much as what me and my friends come up with when we're stoned and farting around in our apartments."

The next step in the process was to obtain backing and funding from a production company, a task which began easily and ended with some difficulty. Initially Black and Gass proposed that the film would cost around $5 million to make, a comparatively tiny sum given the breadth of Black's appeal and star power. Indeed, Tenacious D alone had enough fans to comfortably earn back a $5 million dollar investment. At this stage, many production companies were vying for Tenacious D's attention, but the pair soon realised that this estimate was not realistic for the script that they had written. It quickly became clear that $5 million was more likely to turn into $18 to $20 million, and this drastic increase in costs scared off all of the studios but one. That studio was New Line Cinema, who provided the $19 million that the film ultimately cost to make. "It was too expensive," says Jack. "None of them thought we could do it." New Line felt that The D had a sufficient fanbase to justify the sum of money that they were asking for. Toby Emmerich, New Line's Production President, knew that the band's fanbase would be vital for the film's success, and insisted that it was not trying to tap into the

School of Rock market. "The one thing you cannot do is alienate the core audience for a film," he sagely noted in *The New York Times*. "We'd love for it to do *School of Rock* numbers, but 'Tenacious' doesn't have to, because it only cost $19 million to make." The relatively tight budget of the film did require Black to take a huge drop in fee, however. At this height of his career, his average salary per film was around $12 million dollars; for *The Pick of Destiny*, he reduced it to $1 million, upfront, which he split straight down the middle with Kyle Gass. The two would also each receive 5% of the film's gross revenue after it recovered production costs, though Jack was seemingly frustrated to be quizzed about the financial arrangements for the film. "Who cares how much money I make?" he said. "What's important is we got a movie about the D made, and we got to make it the way we wanted."

One aspect of the film that Jack was particularly keen to get right was the selection of cameos. He first had his sights set on veteran rocker Meat Loaf to play the part of his father in the introduction to the film, an idea he had long ago envisaged. Jack was simply a fan and felt that the two could easily have been related: "If he adopted me, I'd be Jack Loaf." Interestingly, he was not overly optimistic that Meat Loaf would accept the role at first. "He'd be playing against character," he said before Meat Loaf was secured (he had mentioned Frank Black as a possible substitute). "I just thought it would be cool." Secondly, he had hoped that Ronnie James Dio would also appear in the film. They had first referenced the ex-Black Sabbath singer and solo artist in their song 'Dio' from the debut album; a song which praised him for his services to metal but implored him to pass the torch onto its new champions, Tenacious D. Many had interpreted the song as a jibe at Dio's age, but Jack insists that this is not the case. "I'm not picking on him," he insists. "I love him. I'm saying that he carried the torch, and now he can give it to us." Indeed, Kyle went so far as to suggest that Dio owed them a favour. "They've actually [done] some research," he claimed on www.tenaciousjoes.com, "and found sales of Ronnie James Dio albums have improved more than 3% since our record came out. And we're taking all the credit." Kyle's urge to steal focus from Dio might have been motivated by the fact that Dio was actually offered a scholarship at the prestigious Julliard Music School, the establishment that Gass falsely claimed he had attended. Following Dio's discovery that the duo had written and recorded a song about him, he invited them to appear in the video for his song 'Push', from the 2002 album *Killing The Dragon*. Speaking of Jack, he said: "He especially likes 'Heaven and Hell' – that's the one he grew up with. So in the video, he sang his own lyrics to the song and they [Tenacious D] appeared as two street buskers. It was hilarious." On the set of 'Push' Jack informed Dio that Tenacious D were hoping to make a movie, and that he had a part especially written for Dio, who readily accepted the offer (however, it was a full two-year interim until Black called up out of the blue to call in the promise). "He wanted me to play the part of Ronnie James Dio," Dio remarked to Metal Express Radio. "I can do that pretty well, so I said, 'Sure.'"

The film's story follows Jack from his inauspicious beginnings in 'Kickapoo', Missouri, to his meeting with Kyle in LA. Witnessing his virtuosic guitar playing on the sidewalk, he begs Kyle to teach him the secret of his skill, but Gass is too proud and too vain, and leaves Jack to fend for himself. However, that night he witnesses Jack being attacked by a gang of Kubrick-esque droogs and offers his new acquaintance sanctuary in his apartment. Gass also agrees to subject him to a series of challenges and training rituals, tutoring him in the ways of rock, after which he may be allowed to audition for 'the Kyle Gass Project'. After one particularly gruelling ritual, whereby Jack is forced to give a performance to a chorus of pre-recorded heckles while bottles are thrown at his head, he breaks down and begins to cry; and in the confusion, Gass fails to intercept a message from his mother that reveals he is not the respected musician he claims to be. Upon discovering Kyle is little more than a street-busker living off his mum's handouts, Jack is infuriated and prepares to leave. Gass, however, has spent his last rent cheque on a new guitar for Jack, to mark his admittance to the hallowed chambers of rock; Jack forgives his indiscretion and the two agree to form a band. They call themselves 'Tenacious D', based on birthmarks located on the pair's buttocks, a method which the band claim is a highly reliable means of interpreting one's future; Jack asserts that "The science of butt astrology was developed by me and Kyle, and we found it to be incredibly accurate." But this was not the only aspect of the film's first act that the pair were claiming to be more factual than it actually is. The duo were constantly being quizzed as to how they first met and formed, and so the pair decided to begin the movie by putting that question to bed forever. Of course, the meeting depicted in *The Pick of Destiny* is utter nonsense. Gass maintained the accuracy of the events depicted to very last, however, even claming that "in a lot of ways it's almost a documentary" – though he did sincerely claim that the dynamic of Jack and Gass' relationship is rendered fairly accurately in the film. Indeed, when the pair first met Gass did act as Black's mentor of sorts, introducing him to other Actors' Gang members and helping him compose music for productions, but it was an arrangement that lasted a very short period. "I think we capture that pretty well in the movie. In a lot of ways it's a typical Hollywood story: Boy meets boy, boy teaches boy how to rock, boy loses boy, boy gets boy back, boys reach rock supremacy."

In their quest for rock supremacy, the boys discover that the axe-toting legends of old, from Angus Young to Pete Townsend to Eddie Van Halen, all used the same guitar pick – a pick carved from Satan's tooth itself. They go in search of this mystical item, and soon discover that it is safely held in the 'Rock And Roll History Museum', amongst the guitars of the legends that harnessed its power. The museum scene featured the actual instruments of icons such as The Who, Jethro Tull, David Bowie, The Doors, Metallica, Iggy Pop, Pearl Jam and Ozzy Osbourne, but not all the instruments the pair wanted were available for use. "We were really let down by the Jimmies," said Gass, referring to Page of Led Zeppelin and Hendrix. Despite Black's success in obtaining a Led Zeppelin song for use in *School of Rock*, the band were unable to obtain Page's legendary Gibson Les Paul. "Plus," Gass revealed to Peta Hellard of *The Courier Mail*, "Hendrix's estate is really religious, so no association with the devil allowed."

Upon escaping with the pick, the band return to the open mike night where they played their first gig, sure of winning the prize money and thereby paying the rent. However, the original ending of the film is quite different to the one that ultimately appeared in theatres. A test screening of the first cut bombed with the audience, so the duo and Lynch had to return for a re-shoot of the finale. The new, considerably more epic ending saw them battling the devil, who returns to claim his missing molar. This required a reprised performance from one regular Tenacious D co-conspirator – Dave Grohl as the Devil himself. Grohl had previously been offered many movie roles, including *Rock Star, Mission Impossible 3* and *Talledega Nights.* "I've always said that I'd never do a movie, and that's a sacrifice I've made for you time and time again," Dave remarks. "But I got to play Satan in the Tenacious D movie! That's like Kurtz in *Apocalypse Now!* You can't beat that!" Yet more similarities can be drawn with Marlon Brando's turn in Coppola's legendary film – just as Brando was reportedly very troublesome to work with, so Grohl had to suffer his own mini-trial. "Jack came to me and said, 'I want you to know how gnarly the make-up's gonna be,'" he remembers. "'It's gonna be one hundred times worse than the 'Tribute' video.' And he was right!" To make Satan look suitably imposing and memorable, Grohl had to undergo almost *ten hours* of make-up. "The eye balls are the worst part," he said in *Kerrang!*. "First they get the face on, then they get the back of the neck on, you can't move and you're five hours in. Then they start airbrushing you and you're seven hours in. Then they put the ears on so you can't fucking hear, then they put the eyes in so you can't fucking see!" Dave did have his own special means of getting through the ordeal and simultaneously preparing himself for the role, however: "It was great because the whole time I sat in the chair and drank Jäeger and listened to Slayer, Unleashed, Mercyful Fate ... I just listened to metal for six hours so when it was like, 'Mr Grohl, you're on,' I was just like the Devil!"

Upon the release of *Tenacious D in The Pick of Destiny*, on November 17, 2006, Jack Black confidently assured viewers "37 hard laughs, 27 chortles, two giggles, a snort, three mind-blowers, one orgasm and some disgustipations." Unfortunately, the film doesn't even come close to this hopeful tally of mirth. While many of the gags probably *are* hilarious to Jack and his buddies when stoned and farting around in his apartment, the majority of the lucid cinema-going public did not feel the same way. The eternal enigma of illicit substances is that what is funny when high is not always, or even usually, funny when not high.

Of course, it has its moments. The cameos are indeed fantastic, but the first two appear in the opening five minutes, and the third in the closing five minutes. The opener sees a young JB (played by Troy Gentile, who also played the young Nacho in *Nacho Libre*) burst into song for his conservative Christian family, who are less than impressed with the plentiful swears rattling around their smog-grey dining room. JB's father, played by Meat Loaf, responds by belting out a tune of his own, bellowing that rock music is the devil's work and tearing down JB's posters. The audience is barely given time to draw breath after the vehement zeal of Meat Loaf, as JB's one remaining poster of Dio comes to life, beseeching him from a hellish landscape to keep his faith in rock and journey to Hollywood, where he will fulfil his destiny. It's a brilliant opening, memorable, succinct, visually arresting and very funny. It takes a well-used starting point and gives it an absurd and intimately Tenacious D treatment. The final showdown with Satan, too, is brilliant. Challenged to an inter-worldly 'rock-off', Grohl radiates menace and personality as he struts through his glam-metal attack like a towering, blood-red Jagger. Having the narrative delivered in song during these passages reveals not only the skill and versatility of Gass and Black as songwriters, but also what the film might've been like had they strived a little differently. Gass even tellingly revealed that he feels a little sad when the first song finishes – and given that the combined ten minutes of the beginning and end represent the most effective part of the film, there is a colossal, humourless eighty minutes in the middle.

The truth is, Tenacious D's true skill is in song-writing, in their distinctive brand of particularly asinine humour that works so well within its skilful and surprisingly competent accompaniment. But when the music stops and the script is left to float the film alone, it sadly begins to sink. There just aren't enough quality, original gags in the film to keep it alive. The tried-and-tested shtick of Black's antagonism versus Gass' unassertiveness is undeveloped since the HBO series, and the fallout that occurs in the second act is such a staple of the D's live performance that when it inevitably occurs, it feels disappointingly familiar. In fact, the film relies throughout on routines that even the most cursory follower of Tenacious D will recognise as overused – from cock-push ups to encounters with Sasquatch to getting stoned. The whole affair is sophomoric and witless, and probably fails to entertain all but the most devoted follower of Tenacious D – a disappointing advert for a clearly very talented duo.

Critics generally expressed a sliding scale of disdain for the film. *The Guardian* called the film "a pointless, mind-numbing experience", but *The San Francisco Chronicle* was more apologetic, saying that "even when the plot seems to be going nowhere, Black and Gass are likely to give you the giggles anyway." Either way, the film bombed at the box office, failing to make even half of its production costs back; New Line were no doubt wishing the budget had remained around the $5 million mark. Gass and Black stood by their film, however, and accepted the film's failure with admirably good humour. Gass' explanation for the lack of sales at the box office was simple: "It's one of the greatest movies of all-time," he insisted in *The Herald Sun*. "I was on the road and I was asking people, 'Did you see the movie?' and they would say, 'No, I'm going to see that! I haven't seen it yet but ...' And it's like, 'Well, you know, it's not playing in theatres anymore?'... I think a lot of our fans were too stoned to realise it was even out." Black had previously estimated that the pair had one good and one bad sequel left in them, saying: "The trick is to keep stomping on this grapefruit until it stops producing grapefruitade." *The Pick of Destiny* had surely ended those aspirations; the grapefruit had run dry.

Perhaps, however, the problem lies in the public perception of the band; that is, that they are a *band*. Rob Reiner's classic mockumentary *This Is Spinal Tap* is frequently cited as *The Pick of Destiny*'s closest cousin, but *This Is Spinal Tap* was a film project long before Spinal Tap was a band. The subsequent successes of the group, in terms of record and ticket sales, were a direct result of the film and but a footnote on the film's legacy. Tenacious D, on the other hand, are a legitimate, credible, hard-touring and popular band, and were so long before their ill-fated big screen adaptation reached the public. While Black also enjoys a hugely successful career as an actor, fans have always seemed able and willing to separate the two aspects of his persona. Undoubtedly, the majority of the demographic that might be called Jack Black fans enjoys both branches of his output; but it is not unusual to hear a fan of Tenacious D speak of finding his movies hit and miss, or to catch a movie-goer praising his acting abilities but rubbishing his music. As such, when the two worlds met, many were left confused as to what had occurred – the next step in Jack Black's movie career, or the next stage of Tenacious D's musical development.

The upside of this quandary is that while the film was a flop, its accompanying soundtrack was a healthy success. Clearly, most fans figured it to be a follow-up to Tenacious D's debut, and it sold accordingly. The line-up had altered from the first record; while Grohl maintained his position behind the drum kit, the band recruited John Spiker and John Konesky to provide bass and guitar tracks. The pair had first become involved with the D in 2002 when Gass was recruiting for his side-project, Trainwreck. Page McConnell, who had played keyboard on Tenacious D's first record, had started a side project of his own named Vida Blue, and asked Gass to open for him at a show. Gass was reluctant to perform solo, but realised it was a great opportunity to start the band he had been thinking of for some time: "I'd been forming this band in my mind with my buddy J.R. who plays Lee in the Tenacious D oeuvre and, I don't know, it just kind of developed." With Jason Reed on vocals and Gass playing guitar, they began honing a sound heavily influenced by the Southern-tinged rock of Lynyrd Skynyrd and ZZ Top, but with the same tongue-in-cheek affection that Tenacious D have become known for. However, it was obvious that to achieve the robust, muscular sound they were striving for, more members would be needed. After a Tenacious D gig in Columbus, Ohio, a friend of Gass introduced him to emergent musicians Konesky and Spiker. After this pair joined the outfit, Trainwreck played their debut gig at the legendary record store The Music Factory in Louisiana; however, given the hectic schedule of Tenacious D, the band remained on ice for many years. When the two later moved to LA, however, they once again bumped into Gass in a karaoke bar, and with Tenacious D taking a brief rest while Black tended to his acting career, Trainwreck was resurrected as a serious project. Indeed, Gass can be seen wearing a Trainwreck T-shirt throughout *The Pick of Destiny*.

John King also returned to produce the record, but without the assistance of his Dust Brothers counterpart, Michael Simpson. It was recorded at The Dell and 606 Studio in the Hollywood Hills, King's home studio. Lynch would also be involved with the direction of the songs, acting as a sounding board for the band in the same way that Gass had for Lynch and Black when they were developing the script.

The potential problem that the album faces is that it exists, at least in one sense, as ancillary to the movie, and most of the songs were written in conjunction with the scenes they would feature in. How much this affects the songs varies from track to track, but for the most part, the duo manage to overcome this possible stumbling block. Key narrative tracks like 'Kickapoo' and 'Beelzeboss: The Final Showdown', which serve as the opening and close of the film, conversely work very well in isolation, because there is enough of a narrative within the songs themselves to make them cohesive. While they fail to provide a complete arc, as does 'Tribute' or 'City Hall' from the first album, there is sufficient lyrical and musical development to make them effective as stand-alone pieces. Just as these sections represent the finest moments of the film, they are also the finest moments on the album. 'Kickapoo' begins with a redolent acoustic riff, while Black reveals the tale of his oppressed childhood and subsequent rebellion. The track soon kicks up a gear with a strident, The Who-esque riff, as Meat Loaf's distinctively full-bodied tenor chastises Black for his transgressions. The informed listener can't help but wonder if there is a level of autobiographical authenticity to this scenario; but Black has been careful to assert that while his alter-ego's father is a hyper-religious, despotic authoritarian who hates rock, his actual father was always very supportive of his passion for music. After a brief respite, the track once again kicks in with a fitful staccato rhythm, with Ronnie James Dio's throaty howl beseeching Black to travel to Hollywood and form a band. What is so impressive about the handling of all this material is the manner in which it modulates from one section to the next, convincingly lashed together in a manner which doesn't compromise musicality. 'Beelzeboss' demonstrates the same level of compositional skill, and the duo even managed to get Grohl to perform vocals as Satan. Beginning with a chugging, heavily distorted riff, it soon explodes into a fierce metal track; built on Grohl's air-tight drum work, it even features a spectral Theremin line, drawing out the otherworldly undercurrent of the song. Of course, the success of the song largely depends on Grohl's vocal performance, which is impeccable from start to finish. Initially he roars with a vehemence one would expect from the Lord of Hell, but when his performance begins in earnest, he switches gear to a more melodic, classic rock style of delivery; with his ragged yet surprisingly agile voice, he turns Satan into a kind of unholy Marc Bolan, equally flamboyant, scary and funny.

There are other moments of brilliance on the album. 'The Government Totally Sucks' initially appeared in the movie as Gass and Black visit an Army Surplus Store, purchasing supplies to facilitate their breaking into the Rock And Roll History Museum. The owner of the store is played by David Koechner, who appeared as Champ in *Anchorman: The Legend of Ron Burgundy.* A somewhat unhinged would-be revolutionary, he mistakenly assumes the pair are planning to engage in some anti-government mayhem, a fact which they exploit when they realise they cannot afford any of the equipment. Kicking out a "tailor-made jam" for his benefit, the song is a heartfelt condemnation of the Government's actions and motives which tellingly fails to mention any specifics. Catchy and brief, it finishes with a patriotic aria to the Stars and Stripes: the film saw the storeowner begin to weep and give the pair walkie-talkies for free. Sadly, this well executed and genuinely funny scene was cut from the final release and is only available as an extra on the DVD of *The Pick of Destiny*. Lynch mentions it as "one of my very favourite scenes I had to cut out," but also remarks that the pacing of the film was more important than any individual scene. "The only thing that got me through this movie without gritting my teeth down flat was the DVD," he says. It was a wise decision, however, to keep the song on the album.

Other highlights include 'Baby', the album version of which is extended by one verse from the movie version. A lament to loneliness and vulnerability, it is a genuinely handsome composition, sustained by Jack's most earnest vocal performance to date. However, he can't resist undermining the sincerity of the song with an infantile bawl at the song's end, which is either a shame or a relief, depending on your disposition. Nonetheless, this seemingly insignificant little song exists as a testament to the potential of the band; were they to abandon their mission to parody the po-faced singer-songwriter mentality, they might have enjoyed some renown as pop composers. 'History' is a survivor from the band's HBO series, originally appearing in 'The Search for Inspirado'. Galloping along on an insistent rhythm, Kyle's emphatically melodic guitar line underpins a chronicle of Tenacious D's achievements, charmingly harmonised by the pair.

It is virtually unchanged from its first appearance nine years ago, and while it was most likely included in the film as a kind of nod to long-standing Tenacious D fans, it demonstrates the enduring quality of Tenacious D's tunes.

Many other songs, however, only work when accompanied by the scenes they were written for – a dream sequence for 'Master Exploder', a car chase for 'Car Chase City', and so on. Without the benefit of visual accompaniment, the lyrics are nonsensical and baffling, and the songs simply not strong enough to maintain the listener's interest. The bizarrely titled 'Papagenu (He's My Sassafrass)', for example, might work fine as a brief musical exposition in the film, but its kitsch folk-pop instrumentation only makes sense in relation to the mushroom trip scene it accompanies. Freestanding on the album, it is little more than a filler track, vaguely approachable with the aid of cut-in film excerpts but otherwise completely tedious. Only the most ardent fans of the film will bother to listen to these tracks specifically, and that is where *The Pick of Destiny* as an album fails. In attempting to create a film that is part-musical, part-film-with-music-in, they were left with a half-measure that is only half as thrilling.

Fortunately record sales were good, and the album debuted at Number 8 in the US *Billboard* 200 with 81,000 sales, a full twenty-five positions higher than their first album. Pre-orders even saw the album reach Number 1 on the iTunes Chart prior to its release, with the aid of two bonus tracks and short film called *Time Fixers*. The first half of the film was free, but viewers needed to pre-order the album to receive the second half. It was the first time a clip with a cliff-hanger had been used as a promotional tool on iTunes, and it seemed to work, a clever device. The short film sees Tenacious D travel through time to battle the 'Time Goblin' ("he gobbles time!"), ensure Abe Lincoln is assassinated, and get their own back on an irate heckler.

However, the album failed to pick up and sustain momentum in the way that the debut record had and sales fizzled out with the record failing to achieve certification in the US or UK.

Reviews were also generally unfavourable, with many criticising the use of songs merely to advance or supplement the plot of the film. *Slant* magazine's Preston Jones was particularly vehement, lamenting that "once again, Hollywood has managed to fuck up what was once quite funny for a few hundred devoted fans. Whereas Tenacious D was a brilliant parody of the blood-and-thunder metal genre, functioning as a cohesive, hilarious whole, *The Pick of Destiny* is mere bong resin." *Rolling Stone* felt that 'this soundtrack would be a great bonus disc for the movie's eventual DVD release," but also noted that "as a stand-alone it falls way short of their vastly superior debut album."

The song 'POD:The Pick of Destiny', as well as furthering the overuse of the phrase, was released as a single to promote the album and the film. It takes the popular perception of singles as album adverts a little too literally, however, and essentially summarises and plugs the film during its two and a half minute running time. It might not be particularly captivating, but the sheer brazenness of approach deserves some credit and raises some laughs. It was accompanied by a Liam Lynch-directed video, which saw the band watching their own film in a movie theatre, capering around and generally harassing the patrons. John Kricfalusi, whose 'Spümcø' studio had created the video for 'Fuck Her Gently', also made a new animation to accompany the track 'Classico'.

Undeterred, the band embarked on a world tour to promote the album and film, designed to coincide with the theatrical release of the movie. Kicking off at the House of Blues in Las Vegas, they moved on to the Gibson Amphitheatre in Los Angeles, which they sold out two nights in a row. The tour would end in Melbourne on January 19, 2007, and also come to New Zealand, the UK and the Republic of Ireland. It included a sell-out performance at the legendary Madison Square Garden in New York, a 20,000 seat arena that has hosted such musical acts as Led Zeppelin, Jimi Hendrix, U2, The Rolling Stones, and Slayer, all of whom have recorded live albums at this renowned venue. Gass was delighted to have played the Madison Square

Garden, reminding nay-sayers that while they'd 'only just' sold it out, it was a sell-out nonetheless. For the first time since the band had formed, they also decided to take a full group out on tour. Even after the release of the first album, the duo had gone on tour without a backing band. However, the band wanted to go all out for their biggest tour to date. "We're actually losing money on this because we want to do something for the fans," revealed Black to *The List*. Referring to Pink Floyd's legendary shows in 1980 and 1981, he even ventured, "it's going to be better than 'The Wall.'" John Konesky and John Spiker joined the band as electric guitarist and bassist, respectively, filling in the roles they had taken for the recording of the album. On drums they recruited Brooks Wackerman, who had played with punk rock acts such as The Vandals and Bad Religion, and was at the time working on an album with John Spiker.

Much like 'The Wall', The D's stage show was an elaborate affair, with a huge set and a narrative running throughout. It began in Kyle's apartment, where Tenacious D performed – as a duo – classic tracks such as 'Kielbasa', 'Wonderboy' and 'History'. After a rendition of 'The Road', Lee (Jason Reed) spills beer on a plug and electrocutes Gass and Black. There is a huge scene change as Tenacious D are hurtled into the fiery depths of Hell, where they realise they can form the ultimate band. With this in mind, they recruit the Antichrist (Konesky) on guitar; Charlie Chaplin (Spiker) on bass; and, of course, Colonel Sanders (Wackerman) on drums. From herein they give rocking renditions of various tracks from the first and second albums, starting with 'Kickapoo', and also featuring 'Kyle Quit the Band' and 'Fuck Her Gently'. The show at Madison Square Garden even featured an instrumental rendition of the classic Beatles' track 'And Your Bird Can Sing' from their 1966 album *Revolver*. Jason Reed appears as Satan to offer the band their freedom in a rock-off, and is subsequently defeated in 'Beelzeboss (The Final Showdown)'; the triumphant Tenacious D are then released from hell and perform 'Tribute' and 'Double Team' to close the show.

An interesting choice of opener for the tour was Neil Hamburger, who had a brief cameo in *The Pick of Destiny*. An inept stand-up persona adopted by comedian Gregg Turkington, much of his material relies on deliberately poorly delivered one-liners, leading to many observers calling his innovative act 'anti-humour'. But contrary to the stereotype of Americans having no sense of humour, it was reportedly British and Irish crowds who failed to see the funny side of Hamburger's 'anti-humour', churlishly booing and heckling him when he performed on the European leg of the tour. For the Australian leg of the tour, singer-songwriters Tex Perkins and Tim Rogers opened, calling themselves T 'n' T. Dave McCormack of Australian band Custard also performed at some shows, though it was the unexpected openers at Tenacious D's Auckland show that caught the public's attention. Max Tetley and Alex Philpot, eleven and ten years old respectively, were busking in Christchurch's Cathedral Square the day before Tenacious D's show when Jack Black happened to walk past. Impressed, he offered the boys the chance to open for him the night after. They performed Hendrix's 'All Along The Watchtower,' Zeppelin's 'Knockin' on Heaven's Door' and Bob Dylan's 'Mr. Tambourine Man', all of which went down very well with the assembled hoard of D fans. The boys have since been considering various contracts.

Chapter 11

A HOLIDAY AND A SECOND WEDDING

The Pick of Destiny was supposed to be Tenacious D's magnum opus (a project they had strived towards since 1997) and the pinnacle of their achievements. However, it had drastically underperformed at the box office and failed to impress the vast majority of critics – the most successful and applauded aspect of the whole project was the tour, intended to simply promote the album and film. Black was undeterred, stating that he was hoping the film would achieve cult status as a result of its DVD release. Indeed, DVD sales outstripped theatre sales, earning around $9 million. Besides, Tenacious D were in fact only halfway up the mountain, with Jack stating the band were in fact yet to release their masterpiece: "We haven't had our *Sgt Pepper's* yet."

If Black's creative baby was somewhat of an underperformer, his actual flesh and blood baby was proving a great success. "So far, so good," said Black to *Movies Online*. "He's super cute ... He does scream when he doesn't get what he wants. I think that's normal." In fact, one of the few concerns Black had faced at this point was the size of his baby's head. Upon taking him to a paediatrician, Black was informed that Sammy was in the top 15% of the infant population in terms of head size. His concerns were soon allayed when his own head was measured, and it transpired his son did, in fact, take after his father. "Less than 1% of the world's population has a bigger had than mine … I guess that means I'm pretty full of myself or something." In terms of parenting technique, Black expressed his intention to not raise Sammy according to any particular faith or doctrine, instead preferring him to find his own path. However, he reserved the right to repeal this decision at any point. "There is still time …" he told Sheila Roberts of *Movies Online*, "I might change my mind at the last minute and go, 'You're Jewish!'"

Black's final film of 2006 pedalled a far gentler brand of comedy than he was used to, and threw in a lot more sentimentality for good measure. Written and directed by Nancy Meyers, who had previously written *Father of the Bride* and directed rom-coms such as *What Women Want* and *Something's Gotta Give*, *The Holiday* was frankly a baffling choice for Black. Also starring Kate Winslet, Cameron Diaz and Jude Law, it is the story of four heartbroken individuals who are brought together by a transatlantic house swap. Black appears as Miles, who happens to bump into Iris (Kate Winslet) after discovering his girlfriend's infidelity. The two strike up a friendship, which inevitably blossoms into a relationship, and as Miles is a composer, Black even gets to sing a little bit. The script had been written with him specifically in mind, and he fits in appropriately as a somewhat goofy but essentially sincere guy, trying to pick himself up after the failure of his relationship. However, a fan of Black's work is left wondering what he saw in the project in the first place; while he at least gets the chance to prove himself in a straight role, the saccharine quality of the script limits him immensely. *The Holiday* is not particularly offensive – it at least attempts to portray authentic emotional distress – but the neuroses are too predictable, the pain too expressible, and the conclusion too easy. The most praise that Black can be afforded for *The Holiday* is to say that he is the most endearing, least cringe-inducing aspect of the film, but this is a dubious honour.

Released on December 8, 2006, critical response was fairly mixed, but all in all, *The Holiday* did not fare well. Peter Bradshaw of *The Guardian* called it a "train-wreck of a film" that "feels like two hours and ten minutes of very hard graft." Similarly, Stella Papamichael for BBC Films wrote that "the usually uninhibited Jack Black appears straitjacketed opposite Winslet," and that "the journey feels protracted, with laughs scattered very few and far between." *The Hollywood Reporter*, however, was more impressed with the film, calling it "a romantic comedy with a real sense of how romance feels," and "formulaic but with a big heart." The film performed well commercially, though the majority of its success was outside of the US; it ultimately grossed over $200 million worldwide.

Upon returning from the Tenacious D tour, Jack made a couple of appearances in friend's shows and projects in early 2007. First, he made a cameo appearance in *The Naked Trucker and T-Bones Show*, which aired on 21 February. Featuring David Koechner, who Black had co-starred with in *Anchorman: The Legend of Ron Burgundy* (and who had also appeared in a scene cut from *The Pick of Destiny*), The Naked Trucker and T-Bones are a music and comedy act in a similar vein to Tenacious D. In fact, the two members of the band had previously played support slots for Jack and Kyle. Mirroring the path of Tenacious D, they had played a series of successful shows around LA, including a long-running stint at the Largo club, and Comedy Central had subsequently offered the duo a TV series. Jack appeared alongside Kyle in episode six, entitled 'The Break Up', in a season which also guest starred Will Ferrell and Steve Carell.

During 2007, Jack had also been periodically appearing in 'Acceptable TV', which he had a hand in writing. With Dan Harmon as executive producer, it used a similar concept as Channel 101, where audience participation would prolong or cut short a given concept, but it was adapted for a different format.

In each half-hour show, six two-and-a-half minute short films would air, and viewers could vote online for their favourites. The two highest scoring films would be continued in the following week, whereas the rest would be abandoned. Airing on VH1, the show ran from March to May, but was ultimately cancelled.

In mid-2007, the relationship between two of the most significant people in Jack's history would take an unexpected turn, and while Black was not directly involved, it is an interesting and unpredictable development. When Black was living next door to *School of Rock* writer Mike White in LA, his then-girlfriend Laura Kightlinger naturally struck up a friendship with White. They had much in common, both being LA-based writers and actors, and would reportedly chat about ideas with one another.

In January, White had released *Year of the Dog*, a film about a young woman who becomes increasingly involved in animal rights and vegan issues following the death of her beloved dog. However, Kightlinger states that she had written a script in 2002 entitled *We're All Animals*, following a woman's life and calling as a cat rescuer, which White was aware of. In June 2007, she announced she would be suing White in Los Angeles County Superior Court for breach of 'implied contract' (not breach of copyright). The two both claim that their script was based on personal experiences, and have each understandably expressed distress with the situation they found themselves in. A spokesperson for Black declined to comment on the dispute.

Jack's first film of 2007 was to mark another departure for him, proving that even as an established and hugely successful movie star, he still intended to challenge himself and his fanbase. He was cast as Malcolm in *Margot At The Wedding*, written and directed by indie film darling Noah Baumbach. Baumbach had been writing and directing since 1995, when he released his critically acclaimed debut *Kicking and Screaming*. He went on to release two movies in 1997 – *Mr. Jealousy* and *Highball* – and just as he was garnering a reputation as one of the brightest new talents in American independent cinema, he withdrew from the limelight and took a long break. After a foray with TV writing in 2000, he co-wrote the eccentric and visionary *Life Aquatic With Steve Zissou* with director Wes Anderson, thereby announcing his triumphant return to cinema. The following year he wrote and directed *The Squid and the Whale*, a semi-autobiographical tale of fractured family life. It had the critics once again waxing lyrical about his talents, and also garnered him an Academy Award nomination for 'Best Original Screenplay' at the 2005 Oscars. He had well and truly taken his place as one of the most eminent alternative filmmakers in America with his challenging yet disarmingly honest character dramas.

Jack then signed on for Baumbach's next project, *Margot at the Wedding*. He had been receiving the odd "cool offers" for drama, but they were still few and far between in comparison to offers for comedies. "I do it for the love of the game," he said. "In this case it was the director. I really wanted to work with Noah Baumbach." In fact, he wanted to work with Baumbach so badly, he agreed to appear in the movie for free, stating that he would happily act for free again if another project came along that enticed him in the same way!

A surprisingly sombre and melancholic affair, *Margot at the Wedding* stars Nicole Kidman as the eponymous heroine – if heroine is the appropriate word. An acid-tongued, embittered short story writer, she travels to meet her sister Pauline (played by Baumbach's real wife Jennifer Jason Leigh) who is engaged to Black's character Malcolm. She is profoundly unimpressed by the slightly overweight, unkempt and unemployed artist that she meets, and sets about attempting to undermine Malcolm and plant the seeds of doubt in Pauline's mind. Kidman, Leigh and Black even moved in together for the duration of filming to perfect the dyspeptic tone of the film. However, she is far from the spokeswoman for domestic harmony herself, having convinced her husband Jim (John Turturro) to not attend the wedding, affording her the opportunity to leap into the arms of ex-lover Dick (Ciaran Hinds). Thrown into this volatile stew of festering resentments and emotional tumult is Margot's son Claude (Zane Pais) and Dick's daughter Maisy (Halley Feiffer), both of whom are negotiating the treacherous precipices of adolescence as well as their family's instability.

The choice to play Malcolm was a bold one for Black. It is not especially unusual for a Hollywood megastar, regularly receiving multi-million dollar pay cheques, to attempt to bolster his or her credibility by appearing in a low-budget, indie film. Immediately after appearing in *Oceans Twelve*, the follow-up to the hugely successful *Ocean's Eleven*, George Clooney appeared in *Good Night and Good Luck*; after the runaway success of *There's Something About Mary,* Cameron Diaz appeared in Spike Jonze's *Being John Malkovich*; immediately following her success in *Captain Corelli's Mandolin* and *Vanilla Sky*, Spanish actress Penelope Cruz appeared in the obscure French film *Fanfan la Tulipe*; the list goes on practically indefinitely. However, Black had never expressed any desire to be credible in the eyes of a fickle and shallow establishment. He had always existed slightly outside the mainstream anyway, picking films that fired his enthusiasm rather than films that might simply be a vehicle for his specific comic persona. This is a fact that Black himself was well aware of. When asked if he had moved toward the mainstream or if the mainstream had come to him, he astutely noted in *The Independent*: "I think that comedies have gotten more popular, but the clowns have never been that mainstream." However, many comics have made the mistake of picking films specifically developed for them, with each successive film narrowing their comic range and typecasting them even further; most recently, some of the Frat Packers have fallen into this trap, with the likes of Will Ferrell producing a string of commercially successful but essentially interchangeable pictures. Black, on the other hand, turned down the poisoned chalice of starring in a series of 'Jack Black movies', instead carefully picking his projects based on what appealed to him on a personal level. Black has shown himself to be most comfortable in roles where he can be outrageous, ridiculous and half-witted, but juxtapose these characteristics with blind confidence and self-belief. However, in *Margot the Wedding*, he was challenged to portray a character who is acutely aware, rather than oblivious to, his own failings; a character who provokes pity as well as laughs, and who could be pathetic in both senses of the word. But while Black had not attempted that kind of depth before, he was familiar, as most are, with talented and creative people who never had their break; indeed, Black simply had to imagine how easily his own career could've not taken off to put himself in Malcolm's frame of mind. "Throughout my twenties I saw all these other people skyrocketing up all around me," he remembered when speaking to www.hollywood.com. "So I know how that is." The film posed other challenges as well. The script called for two things that Black had never done on screen before: firstly, to cry; and secondly, to appear naked. For the crying scene, Black says he employed the 'what if' method, pretending the circumstances of the film were real. He maintained, however, that he didn't recall any traumatic repressed memories to help the tears flow as so many actors claim to do. "It always backfires," he states. "When I cry easiest is when I'm in the movies, if I let myself." As for the naked scene, it was not a prospect Jack was particularly looking forward to, but the quality of the script encouraged him to put his anxieties to one side and do it anyway. "I've shown a lot of my ass in the past, but never the whole ass. This was a drama ass," he remarked. "You've got to be willing to make sacrifices."

The film is a difficult prospect because Baumbach strives for a realism that is neither simple nor palatable. All three of the principal leads – Black, Leigh and Kidman – are deeply flawed in their own specific ways, and they are flaws that are by turns irritating, baffling and infuriating. The viewer is kept in a suspended state of puzzlement because the second we begin to empathise with a character, we are immediately shown a more unpleasant aspect of their personality. The main problem with the film is that realism is not something that can be strived for, it is something that must simply occur; and at times the character dynamics of the film feel contrived and forced, belligerently pushing the audience from one perspective to another.

With that said, it is nonetheless a well-written and well-performed affair, for which Black's contribution must be applauded. His decision to move toward straighter roles, that started with *The Holiday*, is often seen as somewhat of a U-turn, an attempt to artificially expand his range as an actor and the way he is perceived by the media. But long before Black was wrestling in *Nacho Libre* or power-sliding in *School of Rock* he was performing in challenging plays by Ionesco and Brecht; roles like Malcolm are no so much a U-turn as a *return*. He still brings a degree of the turbulent charisma that animates his comedic roles, but it is here balanced with a depth and poise he had not previously attempted. Admittedly, in spite of his inwardness and eccentricity, he is possibly the most emotionally stable character in the film; but this makes him more three-dimensional as he is not merely composed of the neuroses that seem applicable to the plotline. Kidman also impresses in the lead role, refusing to make Margot easy to identify or sympathise with, and yet investing her with a magnetism that is deeply enigmatic. Baumbach must also be congratulated for refusing to tack on an agreeably tame ending to the story, instead having the chutzpah to give the film the bite in its conclusion that it had promised throughout. *Margot at the Wedding* is acerbic, bracing, mordant and droll, and while it seems more self-consciously difficult than *The Squid and the Whale*, it nonetheless ranked as one of the best films of 2007. Another notch for Jack Black then.

Critics were fairly impressed with *Margot at the Wedding*, and the intensity of response ranged from lukewarm to hot. It made it into a number of Top Ten lists for the year, including *LA Weekly* and the *New York Post*. "I really should've gotten some Oscar nominations for [the film]", claimed Black. "I'd like to play the straightest roles possible from now on. Strictly Oscar bait." Jack was eligible for at least a fraction of the Gotham Award for 'Best Ensemble Cast' that the film was nominated for, but unfortunately did not win. Furthermore, it seems that the sheer vitriol exchanged throughout the film put many reviewers off, with *Variety*'s Todd McCarthy typically noting that "many viewers will have had more than enough of these characters well before the relatively brief running time has expired." Given a limited release on November 16, 2007 in the USA, even taking into account the size and nature of the film, it was a relative commercial flop. As of January 2008, it had made just under $2 million in the United States and Canada, and around $2.5 million worldwide, proving once again that quality alone is not sufficient to get cinemagoers in theatres.

If a picture like *Margot at the Wedding* is about as far as you could hope to get from a guaranteed success, then Black's next engagement was about as close as you could want. As a barometer for success, be it mainstream, cult or anything else, there is none more renowned or widely viewed as *The Simpsons*. Since its inception in 1989, it had hosted a galaxy of cameos from icons of stage, screen and beyond, including but not limited to the likes of Dustin Hoffman, Ringo Starr, Michael Jackson, Aerosmith, Sting, Danny DeVito, Red Hot Chilli Peppers, Hugh Hefner, The Ramones, Buzz Aldrin, Meryl Streep, Patrick Stewart, Donald Sutherland, Martin Sheen, Simon Cowell – of course, the list goes on practically endlessly, and is surely the only connection between people as distinct as Stephen Hawking and 50 Cent. In November 2007, Jack Black was the latest star to be honoured with this most distinguished of decorations, in episode seven of *The Simpsons*' nineteenth season. Entitled 'Husbands and Knives', obese and irritable comic store owner Comic Book Guy is horrified to discover that a rival store has opened just across the street from his own. Run by the even-tempered, friendly Milo (Black), he quickly manages to steal Comic Book Guy's business with his approachable manner and Korean version of Tom Jones' 'What's New Pussycat?'. He even manages to attract guest stars Art Spigelman, Dan Clowes and Alan Moore, all eminent writers and illustrators in the real world of comics and graphic novels. After a plot involving Homer getting plastic surgery veers the episode off in another direction, Milo somewhat slips out of focus, and the show ends bizarrely with a meteor hitting Earth – but then, *The Simpsons* has never been known for its consistency. 10.5 million people viewed the episode, and Black was even named one of sixteen best guest stars on *The Simpsons* by US magazine *Entertainment Weekly*, whose Mike Bruno called Milo "impossibly cool".

Also occurring in November was an event far less jubilant; in fact, one that proved a major cause for concern for most sectors of the colossal American film industry. In their three-yearly negotiations over pay, royalties and rights, the Writers Guild of America – which represents almost all film and television writers – was unable to reach an agreement with The Alliance of Motion Picture and Television Producers, the trade union representing film production companies and studios. The major points of contention were royalties over DVD sales, the position of animation and reality writers within the infrastructure, and compensation for emerging media forms such as the internet. As such, The Writers Guild of America chose to strike, with 3,000 members picketing or refusing to cross picket lines in the motion picture heartland of LA. Many directors and actors rallied around the WGA, supporting their strike and the suspension of further writing until the dispute was resolved. The strike delayed, interrupted or otherwise affected shows as diverse as *Scrubs*, *CSI, Family Guy, Lost, 24* and various talk shows. Many believed that the WGA's proposals were financially inconsequential to the AMPTP, only significant in terms of empowering other sectors of the industry, such as directors and actors, in coming negotiations.

Tenacious D were among those that openly voiced their support for the WGA's actions, and performed at the WGA Reality Writer's Rally on 7 December as a show of solidarity. Black believed that they were well down the list, behind the likes of Rage Against The Machine and Bruce Springsteen, but he nonetheless expressed his concern for the cause. "We like writers and we believe they should be compensated fairly," he stated to *Movies Online*. "We like to ride in and save the day and get all the credit for being good guys."

The strike would not end until February 12, 2008, though a backlog of scripts yet to be developed into films meant that Black was still able to work. He next made a brief appearance in *Walk*

Hard: The Dewey Cox Story, a mock-biopic that took its name from *Walk The Line*, a Johnny Cash biopic. Co-produced by regular Frat Pack cohort Judd Apatow, who had directed *Knocked Up* and *The 40 Year Old Virgin*, it stars John C. Reilly as the eponymous musician. Reilly had been a friend of Black and Tenacious D for some time, as mentioned (first appearing in their HBO series as Sasquatch, and reprising this role, uncredited, for *The Pick of Destiny*). *Walk Hard* is an incisive parody of the biopic genre in general, and Dewey himself invokes and mocks various figures from the annals of popular music history – most clearly, Bob Dylan, Jim Morrison and Johnny Cash. Over the course of the film we witness Dewey's meteoric rise to fame, his first foray with illicit substances, various adulterous episodes, and a whole other series of rock 'n' roll myths.

Jack appears in a scene where Dewey travels to India and meets with a *White Album*-era Beatles. Black stars as Beatles bassist and vocalist Paul McCartney, alongside Paul Rudd as John Lennon, Justin Long as George Harrison and Jason Schwartzman as Ringo Starr. The quartet's accents veer wildly from a passable Liverpudlian to something entirely unrecognisable, but this only serves to heighten the absurd hilarity of the scene. Initially the group appear as ridiculously exaggerated pastiches of their real-life counterparts, repeating their own names, the name of the band, the fact they are from Liverpool, and plainly stating their roles in the group. Rudd's Lennon can't resist saying "Imagine", Ringo Starr just wants to have fun, and George Harrison forlornly notes, "I'm just trying to get some more songs on the album." However, the atmosphere quickly takes a turn for the unpleasant, and a series of brilliant lines ensue. McCartney tells Lennon he's sick of his being so dark when he is so "impish and whimsical"; Lennon retorts by calling McCartney a "big fat cunt"; Lennon tells Starr he can jam a song about an octopus up his arse, whilst wondering if McCartney's songs will still be shit "when I'm sixty-four". The whole foul-mouthed episode ends with Lennon and McCartney brawling on the floor, but the rift is healed over an LSD trip. The role must have been incredibly fun for Black, who had been a fan of The Beatles for some time – though he admits to not venturing any earlier in The Beatle's back catalogue than 1966's *Revolver*. *Walk Hard* also afforded Black the opportunity to share the same screen with one of his musical heroes – Jack White, though he insists his admiration is "not just 'cos he's the opposite of me." As the lead singer and guitarist of both The White Stripes and The Raconteurs, White had become one of the most individual and esteemed rock musicians of the 21st century. In *Walk Hard* he appeared as Elvis Presley, fantastically affecting the King's languid, slurring manner as he nonsensically berates Dewey.

2007 had been a comparatively quiet year for Black – though he'd managed to wrap up a hugely successful world tour, he had appeared in just one film and a few TV shows. Tenacious D had also remained curiously inactive since the completion of the tour, only appearing in December for the WGA Reality Writer's Rally. However, Jack had been shooting a picture in the final months of 2007 that would attract a lot of attention and ensure that the following year would prove to be one of Black's busiest times, commercially and personally, to date.

Chapter 12
STRETCHING THE BOUNDARIES

Black's first appearance on screen in the New Year came on 20 January. It was a starring role in another unexpected picture – *Be Kind Rewind*, the latest film from acclaimed French director Michel Gondry. His career had started inauspiciously, directing music videos for Oui Oui, the band in which he was also drummer. However, his vivid imagination and distinctive visual style soon caught the attention of quirky Icelandic songstress Björk, and she asked him to direct the video for her song 'Human Behaviour'. The resultant promo, an arresting and somewhat eerie manipulation of 'Goldilocks and the Three Bears', would win Gondry many plaudits. He would go on to become one of the most sought after music video directors working, creating original and striking videos for The White Stripes, Beck and Radiohead, as well as a further six for Björk.

In 2001 he made his feature film debut with *Human Behaviour*, starring Rhys Ifans, which received mixed reviews. But it was his second effort that would announce his arrival as one of the most exciting new directors in western cinema, his rise coinciding as it did with that of new screenwriter Charlie Kaufman. The Kaufman penned *Eternal Sunshine of the Spotless Mind*, starring Jim Carrey and Kate Winslet as petulant lovers who have their memories of one another erased, was met with almost exclusively rave reviews. It effectively re-launched Carrey's career as a legitimate drama actor, and picked up a veritable bounty of awards, including an Oscar and a Bafta.

Gondry had next directed *The Science of Sleep*, a self-penned paean to the enigmatic power of dreams, but it was *Eternal Sunshine of the Spotless Mind* that first brought Gondry to Black's attention. Despite having stated that he does not enjoy Carrey in the straight roles he chooses, the film became one of Jack's favourites, and he immediately became interested in working with Gondry. "It was one of the best movies I had ever seen," he remarked. "I guess just because it resonated on a different level. It gave me the kind of feeling 'all we are is dust in the wind … life is so fragile and always slipping away … the hour-glass of time …' No one had captured that idea so beautifully before." Again Jack demonstrated his ineffable ability to pick good directors and pursue projects with a real charisma about them.

Gondry, too, was keen to work with Jack, having been a fan of *School of Rock*. Learning of the mutual appreciation, the pair met up for what Black describes as a "typical Hollywood meeting," though the details of the encounter were less than typical. Black met Gondry at his hotel in LA, where he was presented with the premise for a film in comic-book form, with the sets and the characters drawn in crayon, the basic story mapped, and a few sparse lines of dialogue. It was certainly an unconventional way of pitching a film, and one which Black thought was interesting and allied to Gondry's style. "It looked like really good fun," he states, "But he could've presented me with a turd on a stick and I would've said, 'Let's make that into a movie,' because I'm such an admirer of his work." Fortunately, Gondry did not pitch a turd on a stick. He pitched *Be Kind Rewind*.

The story concerns Mike, played by veteran alternative hip-hop star Mos Def, who has been entrusted with managing Be Kind Rewind – a video rental store with an outdated and decidedly uninspired back catalogue. Meanwhile, Mike's pal Jerry (Jack Black) has attempted to sabotage a nearby power plant, and in the process, improbably transformed himself into a humanoid electromagnet. Eager to please his owner-cum-surrogate father Mr Fletcher (Danny Glover), Mike is horrified to discover that Jerry's 'condition' has erased all of the tapes in the store. The solution, of course, is to remake them into twenty-minute 'sweded' productions (in the vernacular of the film, "sweding" is the act of creating your own re-make of a famous film). Despite their shambolic quality, these home-made mini-films have enough eccentricity to attract their own fan-base from the town's oddball population. Black connected with his character quickly, feeling that the single-minded eccentricity of Jerry mirrored his own. "There's a lot of me in the character," he stated in *The Void*. "I definitely feel a kinship to the kind of haphazard life that the guy lives. And I feel sometimes when I'm in this industry, making movies, that I don't really belong here, 'cos I'm kind of a pig-pen kid in a big industry."

Shot in just under two months, Black and Mos Def struck up a rapport on the set very quickly, bonding over their passion for music and a shared sense of humour. However, despite Mos Def's musicality and Gondry's abilities as a drummer, there were no opportunities for the trio to jam on set, and besides, it's unlikely that Black's love of classic rock and metal would've gelled with Def and Gondry's passion for jazz! However, as the film features the running motif of jazz and its influence, Black decided to educate himself on the subject – which at least gave him a bit more scope for conversation with his father-in-law, legendary jazz bassist Charlie Haden. On Def, Black also remarks that his style "lets a character breathe and is very real" which was an apt compliment to his own "crazy ... explosive energy." Working with Gondry was also a fascinating experience for Black, who discovered he had a very loose, free approach to making films.

"It seemed like some of the time he was the only one who knew what he wanted to do that day," he states, and yet he likens the atmosphere on set to that of a "playground". The main hurdle on set was overcoming Gondry's broad French accent – Black remembers him getting frustrated when people misunderstood his instructions, but his accent being so thick, no one was able to take him seriously. Nonetheless, his first-hand experience of the director only strengthened his belief in Gondry's innate talent. "He's stretching the boundaries and leading the way," he asserts. "I think other people are going to imitate him and it's fun to be part of that."

The film's sheer exuberance is enough to carry you along with the improbable escapade it is based around; the performances from all involved are endearing, and chuckles elicited are frequent and infectious. Mos Def keeps it charmingly simple, really acting as the straight guy for Jack Black, whose trademark buffoonery really dominates every scene he hurtles into. There is sometimes a sense that he seems to be reprising every other role that he's ever played: the role of Jack Black, that is. The first act is very loosely scripted, and Black fills the screen (literally and figuratively) with irreverent and obscure asides, sometimes suffocating the performances of those around him. Nonetheless, his vibrancy is crucial to the film's vitality, and if you're laughing while watching it, it is almost certainly at Black. Indeed, Black states that this was the most freely scripted film he had ever worked on ("it was clearly written by a dude who doesn't speak English"), and given his talent for improvisation and background in live performance, it was inevitable that the film would rely on him to a fairly large extent.

Gondry's vocabulary is really a visual one, but unlike his previous two efforts, he restricts his lo-fi impressionism to the remakes themselves. *Ghostbusters*, *Bad Boyz 2* and *The Lion King* all receive an off-the-wall reworking, and the creativity of the hapless heroes is truly inspiring. But then, it's not Mike and Jerry substituting piano keys for black and white hands; it's Gondry, and there is at times a sense that the whole film is really a hearty, self-administered backslap. But with that said, the film does feature some truly fantastic visual spectacles, all the more impressive for their obvious hand-made quality. In one particularly inventive scene, Gondry creates a montage of various films without any cuts, simply using one continuous shot that pans along an extensive set while the actors run from one post to the next. Black states that this is his favourite scene in the movie, telling Sheila Roberts of *Movies Online* that, "it's kind of brilliant. I don't think it's been done [before]." In this passage Black even had the opportunity to appear in *King Kong* for a second time, in the far more enviable role of Kong himself; however, he points out that this version took half an hour to film, as opposed to the months of Peter Jackson's version.

The themes in *Be Kind Rewind* are painted in broad strokes. It's a paean to the films that we love, and the power they have to bring us together. The final message of community solidarity is well worn, but heart-warming nonetheless. Gondry had managed to put together another imperfect yet engaging winner. Critical response was fair to positive; Peter Bradshaw called the film Gondry's "most uncomplicated" and "the least burdened by the need to explain or embed its eccentricity in melancholy." However, there was the odd reviewer that simply couldn't get along with the film: Mick Lasalle of *The San Francisco Chronicle* commented that "inside ten minutes, at most fifteen, *Be Kind Rewind* reveals itself as an awful mess, and it only gets worse." All the same, the film earned $4 million in its opening weekend, and by its close, had grossed $27 million worldwide, a comfortable $7 million above its budget.

Two months after the release of *Be Kind Rewind*, Tanya Haden gave birth to Jack's second child – another boy. Born on May 23, 2008, he was named Thomas after his father and grandfather, but reports claim that Jack calls him Tommy. Having children had certainly changed Jack's life, and he was more comfortable than he'd ever been with his secure domestic existence. He notes that even before his children were born he was "pretty mellow", but since the birth of Sammy and Tommy, he no longer has or desires any kind of nightlife. Drugs had long since been well and truly cut from his life, with his last reported foray into narcotics being the ecstasy episode on the set of *King Kong*, and he had even managed to quit smoking. In fact, his only remaining vice is "the occasional celebratory J," but he notes that "it's not a wake-and-bake scenario anymore." Jack's means of unwinding had since become considerably more wholesome – reading Sammy the works of his favourite author as a child, Dr Seuss, or making him mix-tapes to dance to. "I think I cracked the code," Jack boasts of his ability to get his kid grooving – and just for reference, the code includes 'Groove Is In The Heart' by Dee Lite and 'Dancing Queen' by Abba. Despite the pressures of his working life restricting the time he had to spend with his family, he remained upbeat about the prospect of balancing fatherhood with a hectic working schedule. "You've just gotta make all the time precious that you have with the babies when you are working... You have an hour in the morning and an hour at night. And you really make the most of that time."

And as if deliberately timed to coincide with the birth of his second son, the film that Black had first started work on four years ago would finally be ready for cinema screens – and it would not only be critically applauded, but it would prove once and for all that Jack was as talented as a family entertainer as he was a lewd and crude adults-only comic.

Kung Fu Panda had first been pitched to Black in 2004, in the wake of *School of Rock*'s success. One of the principal animators on the project had created a special clip to entice Black – *Shark Tale* was released around this period, and Black was most likely not particularly eager to do another CGI film. However, the clip – which featured a panda pacing around, delivering some of Jack's best-known lines from *High Fidelity* – convinced Jack that *Kung Fu Panda* was a project he was interested in. DreamWorks Animation executive Jeffrey Katzenberg had stipulated that he wanted the real Black to be the voice and personality of Po, and this was a concept that appealed to Jack. "It was a fun experience not hiding behind a character voice this time," he said. "You can get distracted by that, and this way, I could just focus on what was funny in the scene." Furthermore, the world of kung fu had always interested Black, with the enigmatic element of mysticism that seems so closely allied to the martial art, and Black was eager to explore that world a little further. Indeed, as a youth, Black had attended both karate and judo lessons, so in a sense it was a chance to be paid a handsome sum of money to relive his childhood. Jack needed little more encouragement to sign on for the film, as he happened to feel that CGI films were the easiest work an actor could take on, likening them to a vacation! The labour-intensive nature of computer-generated animation dictates that actors can only lay down small sections of dialogue at a time, for example, a few days of work a month; and this leisurely pacing suited Jack – and his now cherished family life – absolutely fine.

Looking back on the film, he regards it with the most satisfaction of any film he's ever done, feeling that he made the most of every scene. Jack even likened his working methods to jazz legend Miles Davies: "When he entered the music studio... they were rolling tape all the time just in case some magical genius happened. Same with me. Like if I come in, I'm just taking a sip of water, they're rolling tape just in case." Knowing of his talent for improvisation, he was also allowed a considerable amount of freedom with the script, and encouraged to take scenes in any direction he felt he would like to. The animators did indeed keep a camera trained on Black at all times, using his movements in the studio for reference when rendering his character.

In *Kung Fu Panda*, Black stars as Po, a panda who leads a simple life as the employee of a noodle bar. However, his real passion lies in the mystic art of kung fu, and despite his inherent gracelessness, he dreams of mastering the ancient art. In another corner of the Valley of Peace, an ancient kung fu master prophesies that his most malevolent former student, a snow leopard named Tai Lung, will escape from his detention in a far away prison and return to wreak revenge on the Valley. As such, he declares that a Dragon Warrior must be trained and prepared to face Tai Lung in combat. A ceremony is arranged to elect the Dragon Warrior, and it seems a forgone conclusion that one of the Furious Five – a quintet of expert martial artists trained by Master Shifu (Dustin Hoffman) – will prevail.

However, following a display by Po of mindless recklessness to gain entry to the ceremony, the ancient Master proclaims the panda as the unlikely Dragon Warrior, much to the chagrin of all assembled. Po is initially dubious about his abilities as a warrior and his training begins in dismay, with Shifu attempting to break his resolve and force him to give up. However, Po is tenacious and soon wins the respect of his peers and Master, quickly becoming (when motivated by the promise of a culinary reward) a skilled martial artist. Soon the time comes to face up to Tai Lung, and the stage is set for a clash of epic proportions.

Working with screen legend Dustin Hoffman was an interesting experience for Black. Hoffman was renowned as a method actor, taking on the lifestyle and personality of his roles when not on screen to greater understand and embody the character. He once even famously dressed as a street beggar and accosted an executive from United Artists to win the role of sleazy con artist Ratso Rizzo in *Midnight Cowboy* – a performance that ultimately won him an Oscar. Once again, Black claims to have utilised the not-so extreme "what if" technique, not getting quite as method as Hoffman was known to. In a scene where Po speaks of idolising the Furious Five, he remembers thinking, "OK, what would I get excited about? Oh my God, Radiohead is going to be playing at the Wiltern... They are going to be adding a new member to the band and maybe I could be in Radiohead!"

Beyond these somewhat rudimentary techniques, Black stuck to his usual style of acting – simply getting in the studio and putting himself in the moment as far as possible. In fact, Black and Hoffman for the most part recorded their parts separately due to their respective hectic schedules, and this was an arrangement that suited Black fine. With his stand-up background, he found it easy to summon the necessary emotions and responses without another actor to bounce off, and spoke of the ease of performing in a "space vacuum of my own." However, there were a few occasions when fortuity allowed the pair to record scenes together, and Black remembers feeling intimidated by the man he had seemingly been a fan of his whole life, even becoming uncharacteristically introverted. Nonetheless, the pair got on well, and Dustin even threw a few tips Black's way – "he is the master, for real," Black revealed in an enlightening article in *Movies Online*.

In simple terms of story and themes, *Kung Fu Panda* has little new to offer. It is essentially a retelling of a plot that is as old as stories themselves, one especially overused in the hyper-escapist realm of cinema. An average, typical character is thrown into unfamiliar circumstances due to chance; faced with seemingly impossible trials, he or she first becomes despondent, but ultimately discovers that the strength they seek is not acquired externally but internally. What makes *Kung Fu Panda* special, however, is the manner in which these details are handled. Since the CGI boom in the mid-to-late 1990s, fully computer animated films had taken somewhat of a downturn; the sophisticated characterisation and impassioned storytelling of *Shrek* and *Finding Nemo* had been replaced by a string of uninspired imitators, such as *Madagascar*, *Cars* and *Flushed Away*. The verve and novelty of CGI films had passed, and as Black had noticed, they seemed to have become a means for big-name actors to fill gaps in their schedules (not to mention wallets). *Kung Fu Panda*, however, delivers the kind of quality and spirit that had been missing for some time. Primarily, the script is intelligent and funny, pulling off the *Toy Story* sleight-of-hand of appearing to be for children, but appealing equally to adults. Characters are well-developed and full, far surpassing the stereotypes that they might initially appear to be based on, and an impressive supporting cast bolsters the film's strength immeasurably. Black once again got to work alongside Angelina Jolie (who had voiced a character in *Shark Tale*), but Seth Rogen of *Superbad* fame and old friend David Cross also got a hand in on the action. Black even managed to secure brief cameo appearances for Jason Reed and Kyle Gass in the film, as JR and KG Shaw, respectively; a reference to 1970s kung-fu film pioneers, the Shaw Brothers. Hoffman is predictably superb as Po's mentor Shifu. The very tone of his voice seems to ring with prudence, and yet Shifu has a humour and edge that makes him far more interesting than the archetypal mentor figure. But the show belongs to Black, of course, who employs every exaggerated nuance of his voice to breath life into Po. Striking the perfect balance between inflated arrogance and self-doubt, the portly panda has all the charm and magnetism of his real life counterpart. The charisma between Black and Hoffman is palpable, too, something for which the animators deserve as much credit as the actors.

Furthermore, the animation is truly stunning, amongst the finest to have ever hit cinema screens. The individual hairs of Po's fur visibly shimmer in the breeze; Shifu's face is incredibly expressive despite his stern demeanour; and at all times gloriously vivid swatches of colour flood the screen, investing the Eastern animal kingdom with a flamboyant and mystical air.

Critics were largely very positive about the film. Mick LaSalle summed up the general feeling for the film in saying that *Kung Fu Panda* "wakes up the formula with imaginative scenes, lively and likeable characters, genuinely funny moments and animation that's detailed and beautiful to behold." The movie's performance at the box office was just as positive. On its opening day, *Kung Fu Panda* took an astonishing $20.3 million, and by the weekend had managed added a further $40 million to that sum. This put it firmly in the Number 1 position at the box office, but it also made *Kung Fu Panda* Dreamworks Animations' biggest opening for a non-sequel film, and their third biggest opening ever (after *Shrek the Third* and *Shrek 2*). To date the film has grossed well in excess of $600 million, making it one Jack's highest earning productions ever.

But it wasn't just the huge success of the movie that had people talking about Jack. While promoting the film at Cannes Film Festival, he was being interviewed alongside Angelina Jolie for

American television network NBC. On January 11, 2006, Jolie had confirmed that she was pregnant with Brad Pitt's child, and during the interview, she was visibly bearing a bump. The interviewer began asking about the pregnancy and Angelina's family, when Jack commented that her and Brad will "have as many as the Brady Bunch when you have these." The interviewer was obviously listening closely, and asked if Jolie was expecting twins. She revealed that she was indeed, and that Black had actually allowed what was supposed to be a secret slip out into the public domain. Black was visibly upset about revealing the confidential information, but Jolie took it in good humour. Later Black was asked about the incident during an interview on Australia's 'Rove' talk show, and he simply joked: "I love spilling Angelina Jolie's secrets. Here's another one – she's totally into me!"

Despite Jack's little slip regarding Jolie's twins, he undoubtedly had an absolute ball at the Cannes premiere of *Kung Fu Panda*. In front of the massed ranks of paparazzi and press, he kicked, punched and swaggered, all the while grinning wildly and brimming with irresistible charm. While his co-stars appeared in glamorous dresses and suits, striking the usual poses for the cameras, Jack arrived in jeans and a T-shirt, and was accompanied on the red carpet by a giant Panda to frolic and spar with. He injected the proceedings with something discernibly distinctive – his peculiar brand of irrepressible energy and non-conformist brilliance.

There was some more big news developing in Jack Black's world. Since the release of *School of Rock* and *Nacho Libre,* Mike White had released the aforementioned *Year of the Dog*, and had written a film scheduled for release in 2009 entitled *Them*. However, he had not hinted at any further involvement with Jack Black, but a surprise announcement at the Los Angeles Film Festival in June had everyone talking again. After the runaway success of *School of Rock*, many questions had been asked about the possibility of a sequel – but all involved seemed somewhat apprehensive about the idea. Indeed, Jack himself had stated that he would not return for another episode of the story unless it felt right to him, and all the key players, including White and director Richard Linklater, were linked to the project.

As such it was a surprise when White announced, entirely out of the blue, that he had completed a script for a *School of Rock* sequel. Despite an obvious reserve about discussing the script and understandably refusing to reveal details of the plot, he seemed remarkably passionate about the new concept. Many had thought that the independent credentials of White would discourage him from turning *School of Rock* into some kind of franchise, and he insisted this was not the case. "You want it to not just be a reason so people can cash in," he stated on www.defamer.com, and also remarked, "I'm still, like, crying as I write the script."

Soon after this announcement, it appears that Paramount went into talks with all involved about the possibility of a sequel. At the premiere of *Kung Fu Panda* in Cannes, Black revealed that he was seriously considering reprising his role as Dewey Finn, and had but a matter of weeks to make a final decision. And a matter of weeks later, it was announced that *School of Rock* would indeed be returning for a second instalment, and that Black, director Richard Linklater and producer Scott Rudin would all be returning to the fold. While details remain somewhat hazy, it is currently provisionally entitled *School of Rock 2: America Rocks*. The plot concerns Dewey Finn leading a summer school class on a field trip around the United States, taking them to hallowed sites of rock 'n' roll history. The film will apparently explore the roots of various genres of music, taking in blues, country and, of course, rock.

Jack was in the midst of one the busiest summers of his career as an actor, and had already starred in one of the biggest and most critically acclaimed films of the year. But the summer of 2008 still had much more in store for Jack ... not least another Number 1 Box Office hit ...

Chapter 13

BRINGING THE THUNDER

In 1987, a twenty-two-year-old Ben Stiller was appearing in his first ever movie role – an adaptation of J.G. Ballard's novel *Empire of the Sun*. It was a time when interest in the Vietnam War was at its peak – sufficient proximity had been given to allow the most immediate grief to subside, and the public had become increasingly aware of the reality of the war behind the propaganda and spin. As a young, struggling actor, Stiller noted that himself, as well as many of his companions, were being sent off to boot camps – designed for actors – to prepare them for roles in Vietnam-themed movies. Many of them, Stiller reported, would return claiming to have been changed by the experience, to have been a part of something phenomenal that altered their perception indelibly.

However, Stiller was not convinced. His immediate reaction was, "What about people who actually go to war?" He objected to actors feeling that they owned an experience that was, at its most intense, a pale imitation of what a soldier actually went through at boot camp. While he admits that his scorn might have stemmed from the fact he wasn't getting roles in any of these films, the notion struck a chord with him. Initially he planned on creating a sketch about forgotten Vietnam film actors, but the concept slowly grew to have the potential for a feature. In the late 1990s, he began working on a script; around 2000, established screenwriter Justin Theroux joined Stiller to co-write; and some four years later, *Beavis and Butthead* writer Etan Cohen also joined the pair. It was not until July of 2007 that the script was completed and filming began, but come that point, Stiller had assembled his cast. His old friend Jack Black, to whom he gave his first major role in a big-budget comedy, was to be included. Jack has always acknowledged Stiller for the help he offered – "He gave me great opportunities early in my career before I was famous," he told Sheila Roberts – but in the end, it was simply the quality of the script that encouraged Black to sign up (the role was even written with Black in mind).

The film revolves around a trio of actors, at various points in the trajectory of their careers who have come together to film the Vietnam war story *Tropic Thunder*. Stiller is Tug Speedman, a once-great action hero who has dampened his incendiary appeal with a few too many sequels and a misjudged role as a mentally disabled farmhand. Robert Downey Jr. is Kirk Lazarus, a bumptious Oscar botherer who, in an acute parody of method acting, has controversially undergone a skin darkening procedure to play an African-America Sergeant. Finally, Jack plays Jeff Portnoy.

With Stiller in charge, Jack was always likely to enjoy the process. He would be allowed to improvise wherever he felt it appropriate, and Stiller reveals that some of the biggest laughs in the movie are from improvised lines. However, the calibre of the script encouraged Jack to keep his improvising to a minimum. There were also other plus points of working with Stiller at the helm. As an experienced and established actor, he knew how to tailor his directing style to support and encourage his actors.

For example, Black reveals that Stiller would keep the camera rolling through various takes of a scene, allowing the actors to simply start again whenever they feel they would like to, in order to 'keep the flow'. Other directors would simply shoot a scene, cut it, and then pass the actor a list of notes before getting the cameras rolling again.

The nature of the script – examining the inflated sense of self-worth that many actors harbour – also encouraged those in the film to keep a check on their own prima donna tendencies, creating a more relaxed, easy-going atmosphere on set. It was shot on the Hawaiian island of Kauai, and Jack had brought his family to stay with him for the duration of filming. They rented a house on a beach where they could kayak in the sea. Black was even so carefree as to spend his spare time flying a kite in between takes, but filming was decidedly less leisurely. He revealed that the oppressive heat and nature of the surroundings made for quite a trying experience, and refers to it as one of the most physically demanding of all of his films.

And despite his close ties to Stiller, Jack didn't get it all his own way. In one scene, the script calls for Black to be transported, in his underwear, strapped to a water buffalo. It was not a task he was keen to do. Despite telling Stiller that he simply didn't find the idea funny, and trying to divert his attention with a funny walk he could use as a substitute, he acknowledges that he was simply scared of mounting a one tonne animal. He did a lot of 'buffalo whispering' to attempt to win the favour of his co-star, and ultimately managed to make his peace. Indeed, Bertha – as the buffalo was called – happened to be pregnant during filming, and with many crew members assuming Jack to be the father on account of their "special relationship," the infant water buffalo was named after him.

In a fake trailer which precedes the film, we see Jack's character's latest venture, *Fatties Fart 2*, the latest instalment of a highly successful but none-too-sophisticated franchise, where Portnoy plays a range of obese, flatulent characters. That is all Portnoy is worthy of in the eyes of the industry – dressing up in a fat suit and farting on command – and *Tropic Thunder* is his chance to defy critic's expectations. Unfortunately, regular scenes of debauchery and excess in the public eye have made him little more than a laughing stock, and he is also harbouring a fairly sizeable heroin addiction. "A lot of him is me, obviously," Black commented to Roger Moore of www.popmatters.com. "I understand this guy. There's a little Chris Farley-John Belushi, a little angry Tom Sizemore in there, too. I've phased the excess partying out of my life. But the guy is not a long trip for me to take." Perhaps it is Black's former experience of limited drug use that made Portnoy such an interesting proposition for him. It was with this experience that Black came to *Tropic Thunder*. In the film, the three stars are united to adapt a popular Vietnam memoir, but the project is beset with difficulties from the beginning. Speedman is intimidated by the overbearing talent of Lazarus, and a lackadaisical, free-wheeling approach to shooting causes a $4 million dollar explosion to go unrecorded. Director Damien Cockburn, played by British comic Steve Coogan, is at his wits' end – not least when the films choleric, foul-mouthed producer (Tom Cruise) orders the key grip to punch Cockburn in the face. Completely unable to control his cast, the author of the original memoir advises Cockburn to take his prima donna stars into the jungle and "put them in the shit." A clear reference to Oliver Stone's instruction to a drill Sergeant whilst prepping actors for *Platoon*, Cockburn sees the logic and agrees to go along with the escapade.

Unfortunately, the three immediately run into problems when they are left to fend for themselves in a region owned by the Flaming Dragon gang. Armed only with deactivated weapons and their positively combustible egos, they must find their way back to civilisation, but also confront their own personal demons. Added into this volatile cocktail is Speedman's overbearing agent, played my Matthew McConaughey, who is convinced Speedman has defected to another agency due to the lack of ample comforts on set.

Tropic Thunder does not function solely, or even principally, as a send-up of war movies. It is far more concerned with exposing all the absurdities and inflated egos of the movie industry itself, and Vietnam war films are merely the jump-off point for this far more enticing and sharp satire. Indeed, the film even manages to trick the audience into believing it will be a more straightforward spoof than it actually is: the opening sequence cleverly apes Francis Ford Coppola's *Apocalypse Now*, but ten minutes into the scene, the camera tracks backward and we are shown cameras, lights, and the various accoutrement of the film industry. In many senses, this opening scene serves as a template for the rest of the picture, where it is not film but the film industry that is locked in Stiller's sights. While the scaffolding of the plot initially feels like an impediment to this caricature of Hollywood, once the leisurely first act is over, the film kicks into gear and comes into its own. Downey Jr. is particularly brilliant as Kirk Lazarus, who is so fully submerged in his role that he refuses to break character despite appreciating the immediate danger they are in. It is just because the film is a send-up of actors, and the grossly misjudged sense of self-worth that they glean from their profession, that Downey Jr. can don what is essentially a black face without the film becoming an outrage. Black has heaped praise on Downey Jr., and indeed, it must have been incredibly challenging to get the tone of the performance right. It recalls a brief scene in *Be Kind Rewind,* where Black's character Jerry appears with his face painted black, claiming he wants to play Fats Waller; it is the character's presumptuousness that is offered for ridicule, not any racial stereotype. We are also offered a counter-point to Lazarus' Lincoln Osiris; rap star Alpa Chino, who is making his debut film with *Tropic Thunder.* Initially, Alpa seems like a hopelessly derivative stereotype of a black celebrity, but as the film develops, we realise that we have once again been drawn into a carefully instructed artifice that is established only to be deconstructed.

Tropic Thunder does provide some food for thought alongside the mayhem and absurdity of the premise. This is something Black is well aware of, and he cites Sasha Baron Cohen's film *Borat: Culture Learnings of America for Make Benefit Glorious Nation of Kazakhstan* as the precedent for this. "*Borat* took gross-out to a new level," he noted, "but at the same time he was making commentary about racism and homophobia and these things that were really thought-provoking." *Borat* is indeed a useful starting point for understanding *Tropic Thunder*; the films are similarly anarchic, but both dare to combine the irreverent physicality and shock value of modern humour with more contentious, sensitive issues. Black has spoken of how his character's drug addiction might be regarded as a mere side-note, but there are very few films that depict drug use in the entertainment industry and the manner in which celebrities continue to work whilst harbouring an addiction. "It's just sort of showing this underbelly of the industry," he remarked to Fred Topel of www.craveonline.com.

Black's role in the film, despite being the smallest of the three leads in terms of screen time, is a vital component to *Tropic Thunder*'s dynamic. Stiller's 'going native' parody of Brando's Kurtz in *Apocalypse Now,* and Downey Jr.'s mocking of indulgent method acting, would all seem a bit too self-conscious for its own good were it not for the immediacy of Black's Portnoy. He is a man hopelessly trying to escape the restraints of his public image, but ostensibly too lazy and riddled with excesses to actually break out of his niche. It is the outrageous nature of the situation he finds himself in that forces him to overcome his addiction and become more than a crass and self-absorbed comic. It is also whilst Portnoy is in the throes of his worst withdrawal that Black begins to steal scenes for himself. Sweating and heavy-lidded, he barks curses at his fellow actors before slipping into nonsensical ramblings, ultimately being tied to a tree to avoid him exposing the group to the Flaming Dragon. It is here that he delivers his best lines of the film – responding to a general consensus that Alpa Chino might be gay, he offers to fellate Alpa in the most explicit manner possible if he unties him from the tree. He groans: "Hey, Alpa, if you come over here and untie me, I will literally suck your dick, right now… I'll cradle the balls, stroke the shaft, work the pipes, and swallow the gravy." Black has revealed that these lines are in fact borrowed from an urban legend about Sylvester Stallone, whereby he was allegedly fornicating in his trailer with a woman, but with his microphone still on. In Black's words: "Everyone outside could hear – 'Alright, stroke the shaft, cradle the balls. Say my name.' That one's been going round for decades ... that was my chance to doff the cap to Sylvester Stallone." It is this element of spontaneous madness that Black is able to bring to the film, and with the added potency of his raw physicality, it is a welcome addition to the more layered characters of Lazarus or Speedman.

Crucially, though, the film is *funny*. As Stiller's first directorial role in nine years, it was an important test of his staying power, and a test that he passes with flying colours. The lure of Black, Stiller and Downey Jr. in lead roles is simply too powerful to resist, and the film is as strange and chaotic as it is considered and smart. Due credit must also be given to the film's supporting cast. Coogan is brilliant as the film's bumbling and naïve director, desperately trying to keep his production on track but overpowered by the self-interest of his cast. Brandon T. Jackson shows versatility as Alpa Chino, and new inductee to the Frat Pack, Danny R. McBride, also impresses as a juvenile, imbecilic special effects expert with a long history of mishaps behind him.

Tropic Thunder manages to pull off the enviable sleight of hand of parodying action films whilst simultaneously enlisting their most captivating characteristics. As the film nears its explosive climax, the fight scenes become genuinely involving, impressive and exciting, but there is still a satirical bite to proceedings. Of course, all of this is made possible by the fact that mechanisms of the movie industry are no longer obscured to the public; the film's shooting gallery of foul-mouthed producers, sycophantic agents, incompetent cast members and prima donna stars all come from the public imagination. But all of the leads surpass mere archetype and become fully distinct and memorable characters, largely thanks to the strength of Stiller, Cohen and

Theroux's script. It marks a return to form for the beleaguered Stiller, who had gone somewhat off the boil after his massive success in 2004's *Meet the Fockers*. It is also timely that as the Judd Apatow produced *Pineapple Express* hit screens, extending his dominance over the current American comedy market, the old war dogs of the Frat Pack return, quite literally, with all guns blazing.

Tropic Thunder launched an enviably imaginative promotional campaign in tandem with the film, to both flesh out the character's back-stories and further the potential for satire. Each of the three leads – Speedman, Lazarus and Portnoy – had their own website created, where it was possible to view trailers for their other films, view press shots, and read mini-biographies. Indeed, there are even more parallels between the fictional Portnoy and Black than might initially be apparent. His biography reveals that his first professional booking was in an advert; he was forced to move schools due to intimidation (like the motorcycle gang who took exception to Jack kissing the girl) and he first became involved with drugs in high school. It's easy to imagine Black basing Portnoy's story on his own, embellishing it considerably and yet retaining key elements as a reference to his own past. Indeed, one biographical detail concerns the split of his parents, and their message to Portnoy: "It's all your fault." Perhaps Black was weaving some of his own anxieties as a youth into the tapestry of Portnoy's neuroses?

Tropic Thunder received a good amount of very positive critical attention: *Rolling Stone* called the film "a knockout of a comedy that keeps you laughing constantly," summing up the feelings of many prominent critics. However, many felt the film was, at times, simply too abrasive – Kenneth Turan, writing for *The Los Angeles Times*, commented that "[in] mixing clever satire with way over-the-top raunch and unrelenting profanity, this equal opportunity offender risks running off some of the very people who might appreciate it most." Indeed, the film courted some quite significant controversy regarding one of its sub-plots, whereby Stiller's character plays a mentally disabled farmhand in a film entitled *Simple Jack*. As part of the film's viral marketing campaign, a faux website was also set up for 'Simple Jack.' Co-writer Etan Cohen felt that the laughs were aimed at the way actors use such sensitive topics to further their careers, and stated that "we're really trying to make fun of the actors who use this material as fodder for acclaim." Many disabled rights advocates felt differently. The 'Simple Jack' website was taken down, but due to the repeated use of the word "retard" within the film, many people chose to picket outside the film's premiere. At the UK premiere, Jack spoke of the controversy the film had garnered, saying, "We offended everyone so no-one should be offended. It makes fun of the whole world ... I guess you never know where sensitivity will crop up." Despite the protests, no scenes were altered from the film, and it still performed exceptionally well at the box office. Christopher Nolan's Batman film *The Dark Knight* had dominated the box office top spot since its release in July, and both the ABBA-themed musical *Mamma Mia!* and *The Mummy: Tomb of the Dragon Emperor* had failed to topple it. However, *Tropic Thunder* ended the Caped Crusader's four week run, and after its release on August 13, 2008, it went straight in at Number 1 with an opening weekend gross of over $25 million. It also managed to beat *Star Wars: The Clone Wars* and *Mirrors* to the top spot, both of which were released on the same weekend, and stayed in the Number 1 position for three weeks (the only film other than *The Dark Knight* to stay for more than two consecutive weekends). To date it has grossed almost $150 million worldwide, though estimates regarding its budget range from around $90 million up to $100 million. It is the only film that Ben Stiller has directed to have surpassed $100 million dollars in tickets.

To round off what must be regarded as the most successful summer of Jack's life, he still had one major appearance to make: Tenacious D's main stage slot at the UK's Reading and Leeds festivals. The festivals, which run consecutively over the August Bank Holiday weekend, originate from just a single event:

The National Jazz festival, which after various changes of venue since its 1961 inception, settled in Reading in 1971. Throughout the 1970s the festival hosted an eclectic mix of bands, ranging from prog rock to mod, rock and blues. By 1978 it had officially become the 'Reading Rock Festival', and by the end of the decade had featured acts as diverse as Genesis, The Faces, AC/DC, Status Quo, The Jam, Ultravox, Foreigner, Thin Lizzy, The Police, Peter Gabriel, Motörhead, The Ramones, Cheap Trick, The Cure, and Whitesnake. While it had initially taken its inspiration from American festivals such as Woodstock and the Atlantic City Pop Festival, Reading had grown into a beast entirely of its own, and quite possibly the foremost rock festival in the world.

The 1980s was a slower period for Reading festival, largely due to a Tory council ban that reclaimed the site for development. Nonetheless, taking to the stage that decade would be Iron Maiden, Def Leppard, Blizzard of Oz (Ozzy Osbourne), Alice Cooper, and The Stranglers, amongst a host of others. It was after the late 1980s fall in attendance, however, that the festival truly came into its own, reclaiming its place as one of the best music festivals in the world. Throughout the 1990s a truly eclectic and progressive range of acts would make it the venerable mecca for alternative music that it exists as today. The (now various) stages would see a truly formidable list of legendary acts: the likes of Iggy Pop, Sonic Youth, Dinosaur Jr, Nirvana, The Fall, Rage Against the Machine, Tool, Siouxsie And The Banshees, New Order, The Verve, Primal Scream, Radiohead, Red Hot Chilli Peppers, Smashing Pumpkins, Green Day, Björk, Neil Young, The Prodigy, The Stone Roses, Manic Street Preachers, Marilyn Manson, Metallica and the Beastie Boys. The list is practically endless and certainly exhaustive: be they classic or contemporary, if they're credible (and sometimes if they're not), they've probably played Reading.

This impressive track record continued well into the 21st Century, immeasurably bolstered by the addition of a Northern leg to the festival in North Yorkshire. Despite the rise and prominence of various festivals since Reading's inauspicious start, from Glastonbury to Lollapalooza, to the emergence of festivals on the European continent such as 'Benicassim' in Spain and 'Exit' in Serbia, Reading and Leeds have retained their seat at the high table because they have consistently booked the very best bands around. In 2008, added to this glorious galaxy of alternative music luminaries was … Tenacious D.

The band was booked to play on the Sunday of 2008's event, which fell on the August 24 (at Leeds they played on the Friday night, on the 22). The main stage on that day was set to be a rather raucous affair – with the exception of American pop-rockers Plain White T's and British rock stalwarts Feeder, the bill was composed almost exclusively of metal or punk bands. Post-hardcore band Alexisonfire would play early in the afternoon before Boston-based punks the Dropkick Murphys; hard rock-tinged metallers Avenged Sevenfold would later take up the mantle before notorious noise-niks Slipknot. Then Tenacious D would play, before the revered godfathers of metal, Metallica, closed the festival. Metallica even announced that Tenacious D would be supporting them at a show in Marlay Park, Dublin, as a warm up for the festival – an event that passed without issue on August 20.

The festival wouldn't work out entirely as planned, however. There were already concerns about how Tenacious D would fair. They were a credible and well-liked band, certainly, but was their audience really the same as the likes of Slipknot and Metallica? A festival crowd is a nomadic one, but with a bill almost entirely composed of straight-faced, intense bands, how would the playful and satirical style of the Tenacious D show go down? Even after their show in Ireland with Metallica, it was still uncertain how the notoriously volatile Reading and Leeds crowds would react to the band. As if to compound these fears, there were two major cancellations. Firstly, Avenged Sevenfold were forced to drop out of Reading after vocalist M. Shadows only managed four songs at Leeds, forced off stage due to vocal strain. Similarly, Slipknot – the band due to precede Tenacious D and one of the major headliners of the festival – were forced to pull out of both performances after drummer Joey Jordison broke an ankle. They released an official statement commenting how hard it is to cancel a show, but the prospect facing Tenacious D was far more troubling – thousands of pissed off metal fans, smarting from the sting of their favourite bands having pulled out, at a festival where it is tradition to pelt unpopular bands with coins and even bottles of piss until they are forced to ingloriously retreat from stage.

However, as it transpired, the response to Tenacious D was anything but hostile. From the moment when the duo strutted onstage, Black clad in a wizard costume and Gass dressed as a lizard, the roar of the crowd and cacophonous chants of "D" signified that Tenacious D were more than welcome at Reading Festival. Backed with a full band, including John Konesky and John Spiker of Trainwreck, they magnificently rose to the occasion and became one of the undisputed highlights of the festival. Not only did they provide welcome relief from all the straight-faced machismo and tormented lyrical styling of the day, injecting a much needed shot of humour and theatrical pomp, but they also rocked hard enough to keep the momentum going for Metallica. Opening with 'Kielbasa', they ripped through a set list that mixed old and new. Their show also included the trademark inter-band argument, this time over Kyle Gass' costume. Assuring Gass that he'd requested a wizard, not a lizard, Black hollered: "This is our biggest chance to rock. This is the biggest most delicious rock crowd ever. And you, Rage Cage, have made a mockery of proceedings, I fucking hate you! Of course I want to be a wizard. Wizards have the power to control the darkest underworld magic sauce. I look awesome, and you look stupid!" Of course, the pair patch up their differences over 'Kyle Quit the Band'. The set also included the likes of 'The Metal', 'Dio', and 'Master Exploder' – which Black declared to be "the hardest song, not only in our set, but at the whole festival," saying: "no other band could play what we're about to play, it's that difficult. I don't want to brag, I'm just telling you like it is. It's that good. You peeps that are too drunk to know what's happening, trust me, it's fucking impossible to play." However, the rest of the band leave the stage, and the pair simply mime to the pre-recorded track. It is truly refreshing to see a band take to the main stage as second headliners and not take themselves deathly serious, even daring to test the audience's patience a little bit in the name of good fun. During the song, Gass brought out his memorable double-necked guitar from *Tenacious D in The Pick of Destiny*, designed so the necks of the guitar are a pair of women's legs and the body of the guitar the groin, and Black even pulled out the actual 'Pick of Destiny' itself to show off to the fans.

After Jack's time-honoured foray with the Sax-a-boom, a children's toy saxophone that plays pre-recorded lines, a small chorus of boos rose from the audience. It almost appeared for a second if Black was somewhat thrown off: but Gass simply stated, "they turn on you fast," and a rousing rendition of *Wonderboy* quickly silenced the nay-sayers. Following this, a huge roar of approval greeted the opening lick of 'Tribute', the introduction to which featured a brilliantly baroque solo by Gass. Lee was on hand to reprise his role of Satan from the *Pick of Destiny* tour, and had evidently settled on the notion that Satan wears a smoking jacket. From here they moved into the Who tribute that they had been promising since they were first confirmed to play Reading – a riotous, water-tight medley of classic tracks. Indeed, watching Black onstage kicking out classic The Who tracks, one is reminded of Roger Daltrey's magnetism and confidence on stage – although the man himself thinks Black is more akin to Elvis. Daltrey had previously commented that Black should've devoted himself full time to be rock star, and that his performances bring to mind "that first initial feeling I had when I heard Elvis Presley singing 'Heartbreak Hotel.'" High praise indeed.

But whichever iconic figure Black channels most in his stage-commanding persona, there is no doubt that Tenacious D brilliantly conquered a potentially disgruntled Reading and

Leeds crowd with their charm, wit and sheer conviction of performance. As they left the stage, triumphant to more "D!" chants, there was a sense that Tenacious D were well and truly back on top.

Chapter 14

LOOKING BACKWARDS, LOOKING FORWARDS

Looking ahead, it's far from over for Jack Black. He is well and truly firing on all cylinders from this point forwards, with new projects on the immediate horizon in both his acting and musical careers. At the time of writing, he has just finished filming *Year One*, a film due to be released in 2009. It was directed by Harold Ramis, who is perhaps best known for his role as Egon Spengler in 1984's *Ghostbusters* – but would go on to direct co-star Bill Murray in the 1993's brilliant *Groundhog Day* and Robert De Niro in 1997's *Analyze This*. He had made a small appearances in *Orange County* and *Walk Hard,* but this was the first time that he and Black had worked together in earnest. While details of the film are currently zealously guarded, what is known is it stars Black as Zed, a man who is searching for some meaning to his life in a Moses-era civilisation: "kind of like the Wizard of Oz in *The Bible*." It co-stars Michael Cera, who has recently enjoyed a large amount of acclaim for his roles in

Superbad and *Juno*, and who Black has described as "very brilliant." Rumour even has it Ramis was partly inspired by the Tenacious D track 'Cosmic Shame', which appeared in their HBO series. While Black remarked to *Movie Hole* that, "I suspect he just told me that to get me to do the movie," he also revealed: "It's about ... following your heart. It's a theme I've been exploring before this movie ever came out." The film is also set to star Hank Azaria, most famous for voicing various characters in *The Simpsons*, and Black's old friend David Cross.

In November 2008, Tenacious D will be releasing *The Complete Masterworks 2*, a follow-up to their debut DVD, which will feature a sold-out live show from The Moore Theatre in Seattle, taken from their 2007 world tour. More interestingly, though, the film will also feature a documentary following the duo on that tour, which records – with reportedly unerring honesty – their handling of the flop of *Tenacious D in The Pick of Destiny*.

The summer of 2008 had no doubt been a momentous one for Jack Black, hosting as it did some of his greatest professional successes. In many ways, however, it has a profundity that few would guess at – it also parallels and reflects the nature of his unique talent, containing within it distinct examples of all the key components of Jack's success. *Kung Fu Panda* encapsulates something specifically Jack Black that few have been able to pin down. It is an indefatigable energy, a dynamic passion and verve that invests all of his performances with a very tangible vitality. It is this energy that has made him universally popular with both adults and children. It was not always obvious that Jack was capable of crossing this boundary – much of his early work did not allow him the opportunity to explore more family-orientated humour – but at some point in his career Jack somehow became a sought-after family entertainer. Where the first glimpse of this potential appears is down to individual discretion. Some may say that as Billy Glenn Norris in *Mars Attacks!* he was allowed to explore a more exaggerated, farcical character for the first time on the big screen, and it is this moment that his versatility first became apparent. Others might contend that it was only the foresight of Blue Sky Studios, who cast Black in 2002's *Ice Age*, that allowed him to fully realise his prospective path as a more mainstream comic figure. This is certainly the most likely point that the viewing public first began to see Black in this light, and was undoubtedly the precedent for roles such as Lenny in *Shark Tale*, Po in *Kung Fu Panda*, and even Dewey in *School of Rock*. Some might even argue that from Jack's very first appearance on the silver screen, that most unlikely of beginnings in Tim Robbin's 1992 political mockumentary *Bob Roberts*, Black in fact displayed a germ of the charisma that has made him so recognised, appreciated and enjoyed, regardless of the target audience. What is clear is that Black has become a much loved and highly valuable commodity in the mainstream family market, able to draw the young and the mature into the same screenings. If a further testimony to Jack's power in the children's market is needed, a more reliable barometer cannot be found than classic children's show *Sesame Street* – in which Jack made a cameo in July 2008, talking about his favourite shape (the octagon).

However, that this should be the case is actually somewhat surprising. Black has never exactly fit the type – although the incongruity of his appearance has perhaps been overstated, what cannot be overstated is the superficiality of the film industry. That Black has been able to not only thrive but far surpass many more conventionally 'attractive' peers, scoring roles in films like *Shallow Hal* and *The Holiday* that would ordinarily go to tall and square-jawed bores is an undeniable mark of his force of personality. But beyond mere appearance, Black exists outside the typical in another sense, one which should exist in opposition to his family-entertainer status; he has never shied away from the more ribald, crass, experimental or potentially offensive end of the comic spectrum. *Tropic Thunder* was a film that courted a considerable amount of controversy.

It was a bold move by Black to be involved in the film. However, Jack has always taken a script for what it is; he chooses films based on what excites him, and if that film is a more edgy or niche proposition than many might expect, he simply follows his intuition and goes ahead anyway. Hence, many of his productions have been considerably less palatable to the mainstream market than one unfamiliar with his work might expect. After the gentle, moralistic rom-com of *Shallow Hal*, he is quite happy to sing "Give her a kick in the cunt" in *Run Ronnie Run*; the performance immediately preceding *Shark Tale* saw him kicking a dog off a bridge in *Anchorman*; in *Tenacious D in The Pick of Destiny* we see him smoke weed, take magic mushrooms, have a shit, and offer his friend as a sex slave to Satan, all directly prior to exchanging light-hearted quips with Kate Winslet in *The Holiday*. And so, just as *Kung Fu Panda* saw Jack in a vibrant yet tender tale as a rank outsider who finds his self-confidence and becomes a hero, *Tropic Thunder* sees him play a troubled heroin addict who offers to fellate a companion in exchange for drugs. For every gentle and refined performance there is a lewd or near-to-the-knuckle performance to correspond, and this straddling of the two opposite ends of the comic spectrum makes Jack Black truly remarkable. Indeed, these two aspects of his output are not even mutually exclusive; there are plenty of his adult followers who enjoy his animated films, and even a few younger fans who revel in the particular crudity of Tenacious D's material.

But this diversity within Jack's acting career is not simply an oddity that occasion has allowed to exist. It is a crucial element of his enduring appeal, and a testament to his independence of mind. Even as early as his success in *High Fidelity*, Jack could have chosen to stick with the path he had found himself walking, appearing in film after film as a hyperactive, slightly out-of-touch fool. It was a mistake he made in *Saving Silverman*. Since the terrible critical reception of that film (which was perhaps excessively negative; recall Jack's own critique of the movie as "a little turd"), Black has chosen only roles that he truly felt a compulsion to perform. This has not bullet-proofed him against poor response, but it has preserved his credibility. Even after his disappointing first appearance as a leading man in

Shallow Hal, he plainly stated that he was a Farrelly Brothers fan and was eager to work with them, but had been disappointed with the results. Similarly, it seemed he would put his career on the line as co-writer, producer and star of *Tenacious D in The Pick of Destiny*, yet he was not particularly tarnished by its failure. He remarks that despite the film failing to make back its production costs, he is proud of his achievement in making it. He has never attempted to play games or deceive his audience. In fact, at times he seems curiously oblivious to his audience. He simply makes the films he wants to make, and that is why he is valued above the quality of the films he is in.

This approach has also given his career a longevity that few would have predicted in the early days. As early as *Saving Silverman*, many were predicting that he had reached a height that he would never see again, but he continued to rise by virtue of his fearlessness. He did not shy away from a quieter, more considered film from an indie darling writer in *Orange County*, and then moved on to what was completely unexplored territory for him; in *Ice Age*, a computer animated film aimed at the family market. He was later to effectively dovetail the two worlds together in *School of Rock*, proving that he was capable of adapting to and adding his own distinctive voice to almost any style of film. Demonstrating this versatility without doubt led to him being offered another role the likes of which he had not yet attempted – the egomaniacal, amorally ambitious film director Carl Denham in Peter Jackson's *King Kong*. As if the challenges of this role weren't enough, the $100 million-plus film was entirely reliant on special effects, something of which Jack Black had no prior experience whatsoever. But with his usual audacity, he simply went to a field at his old college, pretended to be chased by giant monsters, and then turned in the most captivating performance in the film.

And alongside these multi-million dollar, huge scale productions, Jack would also appear in more left-field projects from some of the 21st century's finest alternative directors. After the huge success of Michel Gondry's *Eternal Sunshine of the*

Spotless Mind, Black secured a place in *Be Kind Rewind*; and after *Napoleon Dynamite* shot Jared Hess from complete anonymity to cult stardom, Jack was the first to capture his imagination with a new project. Black's persistent ability to keep his profile fresh and engaging by varying his output is the main reason he has surpassed so many of his fellow 'Frat Pack' performers in recognition and acclaim.

And then there's Tenacious D, Jack's band. Their biggest show to date at Reading Festival was a triumph against all odds. Yet, prior to the appearance, there was some speculation about the very future of the band. Black had been joking that fans would have to wait until 2012 for a third album, and even though he had mentioned a new song, entitled 'Death Star', there seemed to be little more information from within the Tenacious D camp. He even referred to the rest of the songs the duo had written as "stupid." However, the appearance at Reading and Leeds well and truly put doubts about Tenacious D's future to bed. On a day dominated by both classic and contemporary metal acts, they not only held their own, but in fact proved one of the acts of the day – they may have provided a fantastic spectacle, bringing warmth and flamboyance to an otherwise straight-faced line-up, but their set was also a reminder of the technical proficiency and energy of their song-writing. It doesn't matter how funny you are, you won't get a baying festival crowd singing along with you unless you can write a really good tune. If they happen to be singing 'Fuck Her Gently', then that's all the better.

The festival triumph was far more than just a great weekend, however. It also served as a reminder of how crucial Tenacious D have been – and will continue to be – in Jack Black's success; what an integral part the project is not only in how he is perceived and remembered by the public, but also in what roles he is offered and chooses. He has always made it clear that the D were the catalyst for finding his own voice, and moving toward a kind of creative autonomy. You don't have to look far to see how deep an effect Tenacious D has had on Jack's career. It seems highly unlikely Mike White would have written *School of Rock* with Black in mind if he hadn't proved his knowledge, passion and sense of humour for the subject matter in Tenacious D. More than this, though, Tenacious D provided Black with Kyle Gass, a confidante, a collaborator, and the godfather to his children. When Gass speaks of Tenacious D being everything to him – his career and family – the personal significance of an act that seems so playful becomes apparent.

Jack Black is now at the peak of his powers. He has never extended his talents so far and reached so many people as he is now capable of doing, and with each successive project he takes on that reach is extended further. In fact, that's really the only common denominator in this random, Nietzschean universe of a story – this "fuckin' empty, endless and mindless" tangle of coincidence and serendipity – Jack Black's indisputable talent.

BIBLIOGRAPHY

Clark Collis, "Dear Superstar: Tenacious D",
Blender, January/February 2004.

Guy Flatley, "Jack Black – Graduate of the School of Hard Knocks",
The New York Daily News, as featured on Moviecrazed.com.

Michael Joseph Gross, 'G. I. Jack',
Blender, 27 June 2008.

Chris Heath, "Black Power",
GQ, January 2006.

Gil Kaufman, "Liam Lynch: Whatever and Then Some",
VH1.com, May 12, 2003.

Duke Lobos, 'Tenacious Buds',
High Times, July 31, 2002.

Dave Shulman, 'Hungry For Stink',
LA Weekly, November 16, 2006.

Tom Teicholz, 'Gang of Actors Reaches a New Stage',
The Jewish Journal, March 13, 2008.

Fred Topel, 'Tropic Thunder: Jack Black Interview',
craveonline.com, August 14, 2008.

ALSO AVAILABLE

FROM

INDEPENDENT MUSIC PRESS

DAVE GROHL: FOO FIGHTERS, NIRVANA AND OTHER MISADVENTURES
by Martin James

The first biography of one of modern rock's most influential figures. Emerging from the morass of suicide and potent musical legacy that was Nirvana, Foo Fighters established themselves - against all odds - as one of the most popular rock bands in the world. Deflecting early critical disdain, Dave Grohl has single-handedly reinvented himself and cemented his place in the rock pantheon. This is his story, from his pre-Nirvana days in hardcore band Scream to his current festival-conquering status as a Grammy-winning, platinum-selling grunge legend reborn. Martin James once found himself watching the Prodigy backstage with Grohl, both clambering up a lighting rig to share a better view. With this in-depth book, he pieces together the life story of one of the most remarkable, enigmatic and yet amenable stars in recent music history.

ISBN 0-9539942-4-4 Paperback, 208 Pages b/w pics £12.99 World Rights

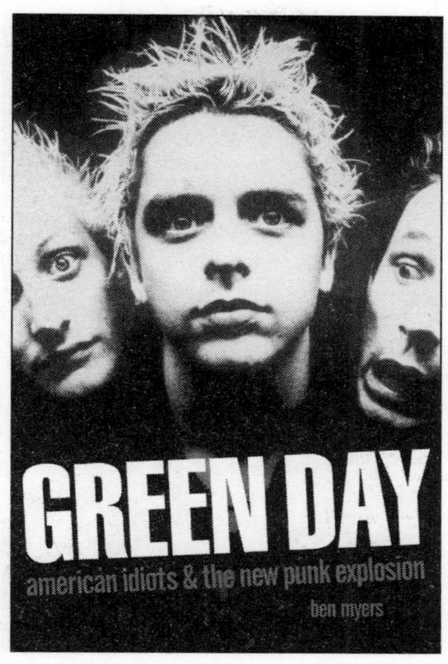

GREEN DAY: AMERICAN IDIOTS AND THE NEW PUNK EXPLOSION

by Ben Myers

The world's first and only full biography of Green Day. Self-confessed latch-key kids from small blue-collar Californian towns, Green Day have gone on to sell 50 million albums and single-handedly redefine the punk and rock genre for an entire generation. Inspired by both the energy of British punk bands as well as cult American groups, Green Day gigged relentlessly across the US underground before eventually signing to Warners and releasing their 1994 major label debut *Dookie*, which was a 10-million-selling worldwide hit album. With the arrival of Green Day, suddenly music was dumb, fun, upbeat and colourful again. Many now credit the band with saving rock from the hands of a hundred grunge-lite acts. In 2004 Green Day reached a career pinnacle with the concept album *American Idiot*, a sophisticated commentary on modern life - not least their dissatisfaction with their president. Myers is an authority on punk and hardcore and in this unauthorised book charts the band members' difficult childhoods and their rise to success, speaking to key members of the punk underground and music industry figures along the way.

ISBN 0 9539942 9 5 208 Pages Paperback, 8pp b/w pics £12.99 World Rights

ROBERT PLANT: LED ZEPPELIN, JIMMY PAGE & THE SOLO YEARS

by Niel Daniels

Robert Plant is a genuine rock legend. Amazingly, thirty years on, his star continues to shine. The tale of Led Zeppelin is central to his life, but that ended at the close of the Seventies – and Plant has been recording new music almost constantly in the 25 years since. For the first time, his solo years – working with his former Led Zep cohort Jimmy Page, numerous guest appearances and his own material – are covered in depth in a biography. With Led Zeppelin he conquered the world, with a close and continuing partnership with Zeppelin six-stringer Jimmy Page he straddled the boundaries of rock, blues and metal; the likes of Dreamland, a relatively obscure batch of cover songs, pay homage to Plant's earliest and ongoing influences and passions such as deep blues and classic R&B; the book also places Plant's later work in the wider context of both Led Zep's own legacy and the broader history of modern music. This is the very first book to tell the complete story of a poor young kid from West Bromwich who belied his humble blues roots by becoming one of the most recognisable rock superstars.

ISBN 0-9552822-7-6 ISBN 978-0-9552822-7-0 224 Pages
Paperback, 8pp b/w pics £12.99 World Rights